Praise for *The Answer Is in the Room...*

"When the well-being of children is at stake, people of all stripes are called upon to put aside personal agendas, find the humility and courage to do what is right, and let go of what has not worked. This book provides compelling reasons for doing this in education, as well as a powerful new methodology for success, and pathway to a brighter future."

—Archbishop Desmond Tutu

"Alan Blankstein spells out a workable approach to school improvement rooted in experience and common sense. His book is a breath of fresh air and a welcome relief from the ideological banter that passes for school reform in the current climate."

—Edward Fiske
Education Editor, *The New York Times*
Editor, Fiske Guide to Colleges

"The Answer Is in the Room *really does provide the answer to school improvement. What makes it great is that it is an answer that is low cost and effective—we know what to do and collaboratively in each school/district we can apply the knowledge and skills that educators in the school/district already have to achieve great gains in student learning."*

—Ken O'Connor
Independent Education Consultant

"The Answer Is in the Room *extends Alan Blankstein's ground-breaking book,* Failure Is Not an Option. *Blankstein makes it clear in his new book that communities can create schools in which all students thrive by tapping the capacities that for the most part already exist within them. The implications of that idea are truly profound!"*

—Dennis Sparks
President
Thinking Partners

"In this practical new book, Alan Blankstein demonstrates that greater student achievement is within the reach of every school. Somewhere in even low-performing schools, there are kernels of success that can potentially germinate into improved practice. It doesn't require vast sums of new money or an array of new programs. It does take a small group of educators committed to inquiry, planning, and action. They will find Blankstein's book to be a useful and inspirational guide."

—Hayes Mizell
Distinguished Senior Fellow
Learning Forward (formerly the National Staff Development Council)

"Blankstein's new book brilliantly summarizes a wealth of information about what works in closing the achievement gap. A must-read for practitioners."

—Tony Wagner
Innovation Education Fellow
Technology & Entrepreneurship Center at Harvard
Author of The Global Achievement Gap

"In The Answer Is in the Room, *Alan Blankstein captures evidence of the school-level success that too many have until now thought simply not possible: When we as adults get it right, students can achieve at the highest of levels regardless of background. Blankstein is right on target that taking that school-level success to scale across whole communities and school systems is now the critical next step."*

—Jon Schnur
Chairman of the Board
New Leaders for New Schools

"Public education is filled with numerous success stories that, for some reason, aren't being taken to scale. Alan Blankstein addresses this conundrum with practical advice that will benefit educators and their students. He shows how to create a culture for success that will move the ball forward at every school and in every classroom."

—Joel Klein
CEO Educational Division, News Corporation and
Former Chancellor
New York City Department of Education

"[This book is] a common sense approach to addressing the obstacles and barriers that often stymie school success. By drawing on examples of schools that have a track record of beating the odds, Blankstein and his collaborators have created a resource that will be invaluable for educators who are searching for answers to the challenges they face. Insightful, enlightening and accessible."

—Pedro A. Noguera, PhD
Peter L. Agnew Professor of Education
Steinhardt School of Culture, Education and Development
Executive Director
Metropolitan Center for Urban Education
New York University

"With tools and techniques provided in Alan Blankstein's new book, educators have the potential to uncover the answers to complex issues in education that are readily at hand."

—Dr. Deborah Childs-Bowen
Alliance for Leadership in Education

"With a new explosion of bad ideas for education reform, we need Alan Blankstein's positive defiance! The Answer Is in the Room *is rich with tools for improving schools from the inside out. Blankstein reminds educators that we have more answers than we think—we can be the change we wish to see."*

—John I. Wilson
Executive Director
National Education Association

"This is a timely and helpful book."

—Paul Houston
President
Center for Empowered Leadership
and Executive Director, Emeritus
American Association of School Administrators

"Every principle in this book is grounded in experience and illustrated with case examples from which any educator can learn."

—Maurice J. Elias, PhD
Professor of Psychology and Internship Coordinator
Director of Clinical Training
PhD Program in Psychology
Rutgers University

"Blankstein knows his people, knows his schools, and knows what brings about positive, professionally driven change. This brilliant little book not only shows what works—it dignifies the overly criticized professionals who make it all happen."

—Andy Hargreaves
Professor, BA, PhD, Hon. Doc. (Uppsala)
FRSA Thomas More Brennan Chair in Education
Lynch School of Education
Boston College

"Another passionate and stirring book from Alan Blankstein! Weaving together evidence, inspiring stories and resources, he leads the reader to an exciting place where it's just the norm for everyone to learn with and from others within and across their schools. And it all starts with questions. So what are you waiting for?"

—Louise Stoll
Professor
London Centre for Leadership in Learning
Institute of Education
University of London

"This book is phenomenal! It embodies everything I believe concerning excellence in education. Alan has documented the road to excellence. I will definitely use this book when working with districts on school improvement or moving from good to great!"

—Deborah L. Wortham
Superintendent
Steelton-Highspire School District, PA

"This book has it right—the secret is that there is no secret. With Alan, we need to shout it out. We do know how to scale up student success; we do have excellent instruction to surge into classrooms; and we do have communities of practice that bring stakeholders together who reject failure. This new system is aborning, and we need to celebrate its beginnings and tend to its growth. Readers: unite with purpose!"

—Robert C. Hughes
President and CEO
National Institute for School Leadership
Washington, D.C.

"The goal of every leader should be to inspire excellence without exception. Alan Blankstein's new book illustrates this through diverse case studies and vignettes. All school leaders should have this book in their library."

—William Mingo
Assistant Principal
Jackie Robinson Public School 375
Brooklyn, NY

"We now know what constitutes good practice—it flows from the outliers of excellent practice already in our schools. Strikingly aware of how schools become great, the major hurdles to overcome reveal themselves. With purposeful focus and responding to urgency, adults responsible for good schools must delve deeply within themselves to find and apply the courage to act. Alan Blankstein, author of Failure Is Not an Option, *once again addresses head on the compelling dilemmas of our time. Yes, the answer is in the room, and it demands that leaders bundle best practice and proceed with courage."*

—Linda Lambert
Author of *The Constructivist Leader* and
Leadership Capacity for Lasting School Improvement

The
Answer Is
in the Room

HOW EFFECTIVE SCHOOLS SCALE UP STUDENT SUCCESS

ALAN M. BLANKSTEIN

A JOINT
PUBLICATION

CORWIN
A SAGE Company

FOR INFORMATION:

Corwin
A SAGE Company
2455 Teller Road
Thousand Oaks, California 91320
(800) 233-9936
Fax: (800) 417-2466
www.corwin.com

SAGE Ltd.
1 Oliver's Yard
55 City Road
London EC1Y 1SP
United Kingdom

SAGE India Pvt. Ltd.
B 1/I 1 Mohan Cooperative Industrial Area
Mathura Road, New Delhi 110 044
India

SAGE Asia-Pacific Pte. Ltd.
33 Pekin Street #02-01
Far East Square
Singapore 048763

Acquisitions Editor: Debra Stollenwerk
Associate Editor: Desirée Bartlett
Editorial Assistant: Kimberly Greenberg
Production Editor: Amy Joy Schroller
Copy Editor: Amy Rosenstein
Typesetter: C&M Digitals (P) Ltd.
Proofreader: Dennis W. Webb
Indexer: Sheila Bodell
Cover Designer: Michael Dubowe
Permissions Editor: Adele Hutchinson

Printed in the United States of America

Library of Congress Cataloging-in-Publication Data

A catalog record of this book is available from the Library of Congress.
ISBN 9781412998765

This book is printed on acid-free paper

11 12 13 14 15 10 9 8 7 6 5 4 3 2 1

Contents

List of Figures

List of Tools to Help Answer the Question in the Room

Preface

Five-and-a-half months after *Failure Is Not an Option* was awarded Book of the Year by Learning Forward (then NSDC), my first child, Sarah, was born. This bald little bundle of joy immediately became my life's focus. And this curly-headed light in my life is now months away from heading to kindergarten!

All my life's work in education is about to become very personal, and I now have the same basic questions shared by millions of parents and educators:

What will my child learn?

How does that compare with what other children around the world are learning?

How well will that prepare her for this interconnected world?

How will her particular personality and approach to learning be accommodated in school?

What negative influences will impact her, and how can I protect her?

The good news is that some 50 leading education experts interviewed for this book concurred with what our own research said: Somewhere within the school or district, there is great teaching and excellent practice underway. The challenge has always been in spreading or scaling that excellence to make it the norm. In fact, many have not even seen this as a worthy goal, and, increasingly in this country, we instead have resorted to rewarding "good" teachers and punishing the "bad" ones.

What I have learned over the past 25 years is that there are very few, if any, bad people in education. There is only bad methodology. Moreover, good methodology for teaching, leading, or organizing a highly effective school can be identified and scaled, given an approach like the one described in this book.

Whether or not we act on this is now our individual and collective choice: *There now is a method to identify and successfully scale excellent practices that are already underway in your learning community.* In fact, a version of this is being used to effectively scale excellence in Ontario and Alberta, Canada, as well as the United Kingdom. In addition, and independent of this, there is now a body of research around a very similar approach that is being used in an entirely different field to effectively eradicate hunger and disease.

Positive deviance (PD), as it is called, was used to eliminate child malnourishment in Vietnam (see Chapter 1) and deadly parasites such as the guinea worm, which "for over 3,500 years has been a major barrier to economic and social progress in dozens of nations" in sub-Saharan Africa (Patterson Grenny, Maxfield, McMillan, & Switzler, 2008, p. 17). In 1986, Dr. Donald Hopkins and his team at the Carter Center in Atlanta, Georgia, set out to use PD to eradicate infection from this parasite, affecting some 120 million people in 23,000 villages.

This began by diving into the community and using a particular process for discovering what successful outliers, or *positive deviants,* did to avoid infection while others were being devastated by the parasite. The second step was to get others to adopt these very few, *vital behaviors* using a particular methodology, similar to one described in this book. This work has now led to the elimination of this plague from 11 of the

20 countries afflicted. Worldwide infections have dropped more than 99% (Patterson et al., 2008, p. 41).

The success in virtually eliminating a 3,500-year-old scourge on humanity had to do with using a particular methodology to both identify and scale a few vital practices *already underway* in the afflicted communities. The community *with* the problem *was* the problem . . . and the solution! (In this case, the high leverage or vital practices included women filtering the water with their skirts.)

No degree of exhortation, emotional appeal, blame, punishment, or rewards would have yielded this successful outcome. There were no bad people who wanted to become ill, unable to work, or worse. There was only bad water and poor methodologies around its use.

Our collective search for bad people in education has left the United States a decade behind the rest of our peers, as reflected in international tests such as the Programme for International Student Assessment (PISA) (2009). Whether the response to our situation is to blame good teachers for not knowing about better methods or to *dumb down* the curriculum so that it is teacher-proof and its use is constantly tested, our efforts are misguided and compounding the problem.

The intent of this book is to arm courageous leaders with the facts, empirical research, vivid school-based examples and case stories, and a compelling process for changing our failed equation. These leaders may be teachers, community members, parents, school administrators, or policymakers. Reshaping the school community and its environs to assure a happy and healthy future for our children is not in the purview of any one person, nor does it fall to someone with a particular title. Our children's future is *our* collective future.

For those with a leadership bent, you will find in this book a sound, relatively inexpensive method for creating sustainable change by leveraging what is *already working* in your community and scaling that. Chapter 2 provides an overview of this process, called CREATE, and Chapters 3–8 provide more depth around each aspect of it. If you are a policymaker or a very impatient educational leader and want to see what this approach is all about once it is fully actualized in a district, you may want to turn to Chapter 7 and read the first case story.

If you are from a single school, you may be able to use this approach without any outside assistance, although this is not the norm. If you are from a district, state, regional center, or province, you will likely find that even with this very specific resource, "All improving districts that we know about have active partners . . . that help build districts' professional capacity" (Fullan, 2010, p. xx). Nonetheless, the CREATE process described is significantly different than the *norm* in education and can set the reader on a very productive new path.

In addition, the nuts-and-bolts practitioner will benefit from this resource. The appendix is chock-full of state-of-the art tools for developing high-performing teams, getting in synch on the definition of good practice, developing common rubrics, doing highly effective learning walks, and embedding the new process (or anything else) in your school culture to sustain success. Additional examples of the use of these tools as well as forums for dialogue around this book are available to readers at www.answerisin theroom.org.

Policymakers will gain a great deal from this resource. It provides compelling reasons for significant change in Chapter 1 and throughout while providing dramatic data around what can and should be our collective focus. International comparisons are combined with local stories and hard data on successful educational paths that should cause us to veer off our current road and advance to higher ground.

The Answer Is in the Room; all we need is the method for finding and scaling it, and the faith and courage to use that method. I hope that I have done my part in making that possible with this book. The rest is up to us all—the larger community—to throw off the failed approaches of the past and jump with both feet into an exciting and successful future. Doing so one classroom or even one school at a time will not bring the results we need to scale fast enough.

My daughter is only 9 months away from kindergarten, and there are millions of other children who deserve the *best* methodology for a quality education today. Now, it's possible. And for me and the millions of other parents, educators, and children involved, it's also personal.

Acknowledgments

The genesis of the work described in this book emanated first from Larry Barber, a brilliant, rebellious, values-driven educator whom I met when at Phi Delta Kappa as a grad student trying to pay the bills in 1985. My work with Larry there, under the direction of Lowell Rose, led to my founding Solution Tree in 1987, and the HOPE Foundation in 1989, for which a friend of Larry's, Ernest Mueller, became the first Executive Director.

Since both Solution Tree (then named the National Educational Service) and the HOPE Foundation were operated out of my 10-by-10-foot living room with no working capital, it was a magnificent leap for both of these established and accomplished men to pay any attention, much less get involved, in this effort.

Ernie had a connection through his brother Arvin to W. Edwards Deming, the quality guru whose work is described in this book. Together, Ernie and I brought him into the education arena, leading directly to our publication of the seminal works by DuFour, Eaker, and others around professional learning communities (PLCs). There were many engaged in our work during this era, including Peter Senge, Linda-Darling Hammond, Ed Ziegler, Robert Peterkin, Al Shanker, Ann Lieberman, and a score of others on our advisory board today. I want to thank them for having made the leap with me as well.

The past decade has been about two things for the HOPE Foundation, and to some extent for education in general. Understanding and operationalizing PLCs has been much harder than has been applying the terminology! Books such as *Failure Is Not an Option* stand on the shoulders of many great researchers, including Andy Hargreaves, Michael Fullan, Shirley Hord, Sharon Kruse, Fred Newmann, Gary Whelage, Ann Lieberman, Linda Lambert, and many others mentioned in that book.

The work we began more than a decade ago to actualize PLCs in an entire district, across districts, and even within an entire province was conceptualized in various settings with the help of Andy Cole, Al Bertani, Mary Deitz, Dennis Sparks, and pioneering practitioners from Newport News under the leadership of Marcus Newsome. Other district leaders who later took this decisive step forward include Wendy Robinson, Larry Lilly, Bob Morrison, Reed Lindley, Cindy Anderson, Jan Nobuto, who served as our first Dean of Faculty, greatly adding to and refining the work, and Anne Richardson, who continues on that path. I admire all who have helped lead the way in this frontier.

The second big leap for us came around scaling and sustaining the success, which is the focus of this book. For that I would like to thank many who have been a part of the creation of this work.

When I first wrote an e-mail about this to Mark German of Corwin at midnight eastern time, I never expected an immediate reply! Aside from indicating I was competing with his dinner out (it was 9 p.m. his time), he was gracious enough to not only provide some positive feedback, but also to arrange a three-way conversation with him, Debra Stollenwerk, and their new President Mike Soules the next day. They have all been marvelous to work with ever since, and the book is only out on this timeline because of their commitment to it. Thank you all for making that leap of faith at all hours of the day and night, for your support, and that of your amazing CEO, Blaise Simqu, who engenders this type of deep appreciation and loyalty among all of us.

The incredible team assembled to do the work included Shawna Fletcher, who did research while driving through blizzards; Allyson Sharp, whose passion and energy can rarely be matched even as she stepped in at the final hour to practically save the project and Carol Wander, the single most competent, talented, get-the-job-done assistant I have ever had the pleasure of working with. Together with Pam White, my loyal 15-year-long associate at HOPE, these women not only helped produce this book in fewer than 3 months, but also made it possible for me to connect with some 50 of the leading educational experts in our field to add an important layer of research to inform this work. Those experts include the following:

Christie Alfred, Principal
Ben Barber Career and Technology
Academy/Frontier High School,
Mansfield, TX

Cindy Anderson, Assistant Superintendent
Ingham Intermediate School District,
Williamston, MI

Barrie Bennett, University of Toronto,
Graduate Faculty; Curriculum Teaching and
Learning and Associate Professor at the
Ontario Institute for Studies in Education
of the University of Toronto, Canada

Gene Bottoms, Senior Vice President
Southern Regional Education Board,
Atlanta, GA

Winston Brooks, Superintendent
Albuquerque Public Schools, Albuquerque,
NM, and Former Superintendent Wichita
Public Schools, Wichita, KS

Luvelle Brown, Superintendent
Ithaca City School District, Ithaca, NY

Anne L. Bryant, Executive Director
National School Boards Association

Laura Cain, Program Manager
Fort Wayne Community Schools,
Fort Wayne, IN

Kelly Campbell, Literacy Coach
and Teacher
Williamston Middle School, Ingham
Intermediate School District,
Williamston, MI

Ingrid Carney, Past President
Learning Forward

Karin Chenoweth
Education Trust

Deborah Childs-Bowen, Director and
Associate Professor
Alliance for Leadership in Education,
Samford University

Jonathan Cohen, President
National School Climate Center and
Adjunct Professor, Psychology and
Education, Teachers College, Columbia
University

Gail M. Cooper, Principal
Pottstown Middle School, Pottstown, PA

Ronald F. Cornelison, Chairman
America's Leading Judicial Solutions
Provider (AMCAD®)

Linda Darling-Hammond, Charles E.
Ducommun Professor of Education
Stanford University

Harriett Diaz, Principal
Renaissance Middle School, Queens, NY

Mary E. Dietz, International
Consultant
Frameworks for Learning Organizations

Tania Dupuis, Assistant Principal
Williamston Middle School, Ingham
Intermediate School District,
Williamston, MI

John Q. Easton, Director
Institute of Education Sciences

Maurice J. Elias, Professor of Psychology
and Internship Coordinator/Director of
Clinical Training, Ph.D. Program in
Psychology, Rutgers University and
Academic Director, Rutgers Civic
Engagement and Service Education
Partnerships Program Coordinator,
Improving School Climate for Academic
and Life Success (ISCALS), Rutgers Center
for Applied Psychology

Richard F. Elmore, Gregory Anrig
Professor of Educational
Leadership
Harvard Graduate School of Education

Edward Fiske, Education Editor
The New York Times and Editor,
Fiske Guide to Colleges

Seymour Fliegel, President
Center for Educational Innovation—
Public Education Association

Avis Glaze, President
Edu-Quest International, Inc. and Former
Chief Student Achievement Officer of
Ontario

Erin Gruwell, President
Freedom Writers Foundation

Thomas R. Guskey, Professor
Department of Educational, School and
Counseling Psychology, College of
Education, University of Kentucky

Andrew Hargreaves, Professor, B.A., Ph.D.,
Hon. Doc. (Uppsala), FRSA Thomas More
Brennan Chair in Education and Lynch
School of Education

Laura Hill, Teacher
Williamston Middle School, Ingham
Intermediate School District,
Williamston, MI

Stephanie Hirsh, Executive Director
Learning Forward, formerly the National
Staff Development Council

Paul Houston, President
Center for Empowered Leadership and
Executive Director, Emeritus, American
Association of School Administrators

Robert C. Hughes, President and CEO
National Institute for School Leadership

Mary Ellen Isaac, Former Chief Academic
Officer, Wichita Public Schools and
currently Vice President of the Leadership
Institute at the Schultz Center for Teaching
and Leadership

Sarah Jandrucko, Area Superintendent
Mansfield Independent School District,
Mansfield, TX

Wendell Joubert, Interim Principal
Rogene Worley Middle School, Mansfield
Independent School District,
Mansfield, TX

Joell Klein, CEO Educational Division
News Corporation and Former Chancellor,
New York City Department of Education

Michael S. Knapp, Professor
Educational Leadership & Policy Studies,
College of Education, University of
Washington

Stanley Kogut, Superintendent
Ingham Intermediate School District,
Williamston, MI

Linda Lambert, Professor Emeritus
California State University, East Bay/
International Consultant in Leadership
and full-time author

Karen Seashore Louis, Regents Professor
of Organizational Leadership, Policy and
Development and Robert H. Beck Chair of
Ideas in Education

Scott Martin, Principal
Williamston Middle School, Ingham
Intermediate School District,
Williamston, MI

E. Kent Martz, Principal
Waynedale Elementary School, Fort
Wayne, IN

Jay McTighe, Education
Consultant
Jay McTighe & Associates

William Mingo, Assistant Principal
Jackie Robinson Public School 375,
Brooklyn, NY

Hayes Mizell, Distinguished
Senior Fellow
Learning Forward/National Staff
Development Council

Bob Morrison, Superintendent
Mansfield Independent School District,
Mansfield, TX

Narda Murphy, Superintendent
Williamston Community Schools,
Williamston, MI

Pedro A. Noguera, Peter L. Agnew
Professor of Education
Steinhardt School of Culture, Education
and Development and Executive Director,
Metropolitan Center for Urban Education,
New York University

Ken O'Connor, Education Consultant
Assess for Success Consulting, Toronto,
Canada

Bradley Portin, Director and
Professor
Education Program, University of
Washington Bothell

Carolyn Powers, Director of Elementary
Administration
Fort Wayne Community Schools, Fort
Wayne, IN

Mel Riddile, Associate Director for High
School Services
National Association of Secondary School
Principals

Wendy Robinson, Superintendent
Fort Wayne Community Schools, Fort
Wayne, IN

Charles Saylors, President
National Parent Teacher Association

Phillip Schlechty, Founder
and CEO
Schlechty Center

Jon Schnur, Chairman of
the Board
New Leaders for New Schools

Denise Seguine, Chief Academic
Officer
Wichita Public Schools,
Wichita, KS

Christine Sermak, Former Principal
Williamston Middle School, Ingham
Intermediate School District,
Williamston, MI

Nancy Shin, Executive Director
HOPE Foundation

Dennis Shirley, Professor
Department of Teacher Education, Special
Education, Curriculum and Instruction,
Lynch School of Education, Boston
College

Jason Short, Principal
Asa E. Low Jr. Intermediate School,
Mansfield Independent School District,
Mansfield, TX

Shawn Smiley, Principal
Willard Shambaugh Elementary School,
Fort Wayne Community Schools, Fort
Wayne, IN

Dennis Sparks, Emeritus Executive
Director
National Staff Development Council

Monique Sternin, Adjunct Associate
Professor
Tufts University Friedman School of
Nutrition Science and Policy and Senior
Advisor, Positive Deviance Initiative

Krista Stockman, Public Information
Officer
Fort Wayne Community Schools,
Fort Wayne, IN

Louise Stoll, Professor
London Centre for Leadership in Learning,
Institute of Education, University of
London

Maurice Sykes, Executive Director
Early Childhood Leadership Institute

Marcia Tate, Education Consultant, Author,
CEO
Developing Minds, Inc.

Archbishop Desmond Tutu

Dennis Van Roekel, President
National Education Association

Jim Vaszauskas, Associate Superintendent
Curriculum, Instruction and
Accountability, Mansfield Independent
School District, Mansfield, TX

Tony Wagner, Innovation Education
Fellow/Technology & Entrepreneurship
Center, Harvard School of Engineering &
Applied Sciences
Author, *The Global Achievement Gap*

Tom Watts, Director of Exceptional
Education TST BOCES

Gene Wilhoit, Executive Director
Council of Chief State School Officers

Cheryl Scott Williams, Executive Director
Learning First Alliance

John I. Wilson, Executive Director
National Education Association

Marion Wilson, Principal
Jackie Robinson Public School 375,
Brooklyn, NY

Deborah L. Wortham, CEO
Wortham Educational Associates

Hearing from each of you was exhilarating and humbling for me. I am deeply grateful to each of you for having taken the time to help advance what we can accomplish on behalf of our students.

About the Author

Alan M. Blankstein is Founder and President of the HOPE (Harnessing Optimism and Potential through Education) Foundation, a not-for-profit organization, the Honorary Chair of which is Nobel Prize winner Archbishop Desmond Tutu. The HOPE Foundation is dedicated to supporting educational leaders over time in creating school cultures where failure is not an option for *any* student. Founded in 1989, the HOPE Foundation has focused for the past decade on helping districts build leadership capacity to close gaps and sustain student success.

The HOPE Foundation launched the professional learning communities movement in educational circles, first by bringing W. Edwards Deming and later Peter Senge to light in a series of Shaping America's Future forums and PBS video conferences from 1989 to 1992. The HOPE Foundation now provides some 20 conferences annually, highlighting their long-term successes in sustaining student achievement in districts and regions in 37 states and parts of Canada and South Africa.

A former "high-risk" youth, Alan began his career in education as a music teacher and has worked in youth-serving organizations since 1983, including the March of Dimes, Phi Delta Kappa, and the National Educational Service (now Solution Tree), which he founded in 1987 and directed for 12 years.

In addition to authorship of this award-winning book, Alan is publisher of three *Failure Is Not an Option* video series and, with Paul Houston, is senior editor of the 13-volume *The Soul of Educational Leadership* series. Alan also coauthored the *Reaching Today's Youth* curriculum and has published articles in *Educational Leadership, The School Administrator, Executive Educator, High School Magazine, Reaching Today's Youth,* and *Inside the Workshop.* Alan has also provided keynote presentations and workshops for virtually every major educational organization.

Alan served on the Harvard International Principals Centers advisory board, as board member for Federation of Families for Children's Mental Health, as Co-Chair of Indiana University's Neal Marshall Black Culture Center's Community Network, and as advisor to the Faculty and Staff for Student Excellence (FASE) mentoring program. He also served as advisory board member for the Forum on Race, Equity, and Human Understanding with the Monroe County Schools in Indiana and on the Board of Trustees for the Jewish Child Care Agency (JCCA), in which he was once a youth in residence.

Dedication

Echoes roll from soul to soul, and grow forever and ever.

—Alfred Tennyson

*T*he Answer Is in the Room was written to help individuals rediscover and reclaim their power to affect change. It is easy to become overwhelmed by the inexorable forces that seem to control our individual and collective directions in life. Yet rather than succumb to these strong currents, this book is about a process for shifting them. It is dedicated, therefore, to four people whom I have known who have had such an impact as well:

To my dearest great Aunt Edna who died while I was completing this work, I dedicate this book. In both her personal life and her profession in social work, she had the courage of a small army and always rooted herself in justice and the fight for the underdog. She believed in me and supported me at crucial junctures, greatly impacting the outcome of the situation and trajectory of my life.

To my best friend and colleague of 22 years, Nancy Shin-Pascal, I dedicate this book. Through her tireless commitment to the work described in this book, she has saved many lives and enhanced the lives of millions of children directly and through the ripple effect described by Tennyson above. Most of all, I thank her for being there for me.

To Dr. Myland Brown, whose profession it was to find promising, yet challenged youth like myself, and give them a shot at college, I dedicate this book. Had he not included me on the list of EOP grant recipients and then nurtured me and our relationship moving forward, I would likely not be writing anything other than graffiti in Queens, New York, right now!

To W. Edwards Deming, whose powerful and practical concepts and curmudgeonly delivery of them made him instantly among my favorite people in the world, I dedicate this book. He was also kind and courageous enough to mentor me when I was just a 20-something pipsqueak, which in turn altered my view of everything, and serves as a foundation for this book.

Why We Can't Wait to Scale Student Success

"We can, whenever and wherever we choose, successfully teach all children whose schooling is of interest to us. We already know more than we need to in order to do that. Whether or not we do it must finally depend upon how we feel about the fact that we haven't so far."

—Ron Edmonds, Founder
Effective Schools Movement, 1970

"Ninety percent of the work we use is American research ... you've got the best research in the world ... but, you don't apply it."

—Barrie Bennett, Associate Professor
Ontario Institute for Studies in Education
University of Toronto, Canada

"In the end it is clear: There is going to be the need to rally leadership from across education and other sectors to put education first—to do whatever it takes to help get all of our kids much better results and outcomes than we ever have before."

—Jonathan Schnur, CEO
New Leaders for New Schools

THE POWER OF POSITIVE DEVIANCE SAVES MILLIONS OF CHILDREN IN VIETNAM

On April 29, 1975, the official American presence in Saigon ended. The last Americans were evacuated by helicopter from the U.S. embassy rooftop, and within hours the Saigon government surrendered to the Viet Cong.

As with many conflicts, it is the children who suffer most, and some 25 years later, in 1990, about 65 percent of all Vietnamese children experienced malnutrition (Singhal, Sternin, & Dura, 2009). Although this was a horrendous situation, it was about to get worse, as the health care system was near collapse because of a privatization plan absolving the government from responsibility.

In the country's desperation, the Vietnamese government issued the United States' nongovernmental organization (NGO), Save the Children, an invitation to create an approach to help eradicate childhood malnutrition in the country's poor villages. Jerry Sternin, then director of Save the Children's Philippines program, eagerly accepted and moved to Hanoi with his wife, Monique, and 10-year-old son, Sam, in December 1990. In addition to the daunting challenge of eradicating decades of intergenerational poverty and malnutrition in a country whose infrastructure and economy were devastated by war, Sternin was met with great distrust and even contempt, because of his affiliation with an American NGO (Pascale, Sternin, & Sternin, 2010). These sentiments culminated in a brief meeting with an official at the Ministry of Foreign Affairs who told Sternin that he had only 6 months to demonstrate impact or leave the country (Pascale et al.).

Needing to quickly affect meaningful change in a situation that had been intractable for decades, Jerry thought back to a concept that had been around for years and had been published in 1989 by Marian Zeitlin and colleagues from Tufts University called positive deviance (PD) (Pascale et al., 2010). It described how there were often outliers in poor families; some children who managed to remain relatively well-nourished even when children and families around them could not. These children were termed "Positive Deviants" (Pascale et al.).

Sternin devised a plan to systematically *scale* PD using a subsection of the population needing intervention. The concept was simple: Find those families whose children were thriving while those around them were going hungry, study how they achieved their successes, and then spread those practices throughout the community. Yet the implementation of this idea was fraught with social and other challenges, especially since it could easily be seen as coming from outsiders—potentially hostile ones at that!

At the end of the 6-month period, there was a literal *weighing in* of children who would determine the fate of the program and ultimately the lives of millions in Vietnam. The initial 6 months led to a 40% reduction of malnutrition among those in the program. In 2 years, malnourishment was eradicated among the villages that were the focus for this work. Over the next 7 years, 50,000 children were saved, and eventually the program reached more than 2 million people (Pascale et al., 2010).

APPLYING POSITIVE DEVIANCE TO EDUCATION

The power of this concept for educational change is enormous. Assuming it could apply in an educational context, it would be possible to change practice exponentially—not just one school at a time. It could empower all those involved, since the process is based on what ordinary people are already doing well. The cost for implementation would be minimal since it builds on practice already in existence and leverages the knowledge and skills of practitioners as the experts.

There is excellence in every school—right next door to substandard practices. However, the practices of the effective teachers aren't naturally spreading to others—not even to those across the hall. Why is this? Consider this exchange following a presentation in one U.S. high school.

High school teacher: "That all sounds good, but how do you propose we teach those kids who just don't want to learn?!"

I provided neither an argument nor an answer—either of which may have been what he wanted. Instead, I asked him and his peers this question:

"Is there anyone in the school building who is succeeding with those same students that you feel don't want to learn?" While he slowly shook his head *no*, everyone else in the audience nodded their heads *yes*.

There Is a Better Way

The above disparity of practice within the school is not unusual in our experience. In every single school the HOPE Foundation has worked in—no matter how poor or underperforming—there have been pockets of excellence. Among the almost 50 leading researchers and educational leaders from North America and the United Kingdom interviewed for this book, including pioneers working in the lowest performing schools and districts nationally, virtually all believed there were pockets of excellent practice within almost any given school. Although there is presumably excellence in any school in the United States, and throughout the world for that matter, why isn't it being brought to scale?

According to Pascale and colleagues (2010), the PD approach used in Vietnam has been used effectively in various educational settings in 31 nations in Africa, 10 in Asia, 5 in Latin America, and in dozens of applications within the United States and Canada. Although *made in America,* PD is being used much more prolifically throughout the world than in the United States. And except for a relatively few pioneering districts, including those in this book, it is not systematically used in U.S. education. Many reasons for this exist, some of which are outlined in the section that follows. Let's start with what we *can* do and what is *already working* first.

GOOD NEWS FOR SCALING STUDENT SUCCESS

We have learned some very exciting things in education over the past decade. In general, we know what it takes to turn around a low-performing school, and several examples from schools being dramatically improved using *Failure Is Not an Option®: 6 Principles That Guide Student Achievement in High-Performing Schools* as their basis are provided in this book. We now also know how to scale excellent practices across an entire school district or region using the researched-based process described in this resource.

The process leverages and brings to scale what is already working in the school community. Therefore, it can be done for a fraction of the cost of almost any other professional development. And since it is an *inside-out* approach, the school community owns and sustains the successes and the capacity and process for continually improving. In essence, this process is based on one simple principle: The answer is in the room. The process of identifying the answer and scaling success is the question and focus of this book.

The most recent iteration of this approach in education, often referred to as "Networks," or "Communities of Practice," was first piloted and shown effective more than a decade ago. Several countries—notably the United Kingdom and two provinces in Canada—have come to provide systemic support for these ideas. In *All Systems Go,* Fullan estimates about 5% of the United States has adopted this process while the country as a whole has continued along a much less productive path (Fullan, 2010). These pioneering U.S. districts include Fort Wayne, Indiana; Mattoon, Illinois; Mansfield, Texas; Pottstown, Pennsylvania; and Wichita, Kansas. The HOPE Foundation is aware of more than 250 schools in 10 districts, as well as 30 independent schools, using this process in order to scale student success.

ABOUT THIS BOOK AND CHAPTER

This book, therefore, has two aims. The first is to help those educators, policymakers, researchers, and concerned community members who don't believe that the answer is in the room to at least consider the possibility long enough to explore, if not support, it and the extraordinary outcomes it can yield. The second is to assist those educational leaders and practitioners to advance their ability to scale successes already in their schools. Whereas *Failure Is Not an Option* provides six principles as a system and framework for action, as well as strategies and tactics for proceeding, *The Answer Is in the Room* overviews a powerful process for using those tools.

NOTE TO READER: To get a quick, specific example of how this process plays itself out in a school, turn to Chapter 7 and read "Case Story Part 1."

This resource also takes us across the globe to school-based practices as well as to successes in eradicating famine and disease in Vietnam and sub-Saharan Africa using a process similar to that which we have used to scale school successes. Although early uses of pairing schools, or *networking* as described in this book, were arguably piloted in the United States*(A. Hargreaves, personal communication, December 2010; Hargreaves, 2004; Hargreaves & Fink, 2006), it has become a fulcrum for change in other parts of the world, notably the U.K. where it receives government support (A. Hargreaves, personal communication, 2010) and in Ontario, Canada, where the province is using it as a major strategy for its systemic improvement (Fullan, 2010).

Note: Louise Stoll shares that "networks" have been around in the United Kingdom for decades, and Linda Lambert references Ann Lieberman among the early pioneers.

The results we have seen from scaling positive deviance through networking in the United States alone over the past 3 years are significant:

- Three New York City schools went from being on the verge of closing down to being rated by the New York Board of Education as "A" schools.
- Wichita Public Schools used this process in half of their 88 schools for the first year. There were 15 schools that made annual yearly progress (AYP) in that year that had not in prior years, and 12 of those were in the cohort using the process. Wichita Public Schools also narrowed the achievement gap between Caucasian and African-American students, and exceeded the state's graduation target.
- Fort Wayne Public Schools is one of only 70 systems in the entire country required to make progress in 37 subcategories of students in order to make AYP, and they succeeded in advancing in all 37 categories. All this during a year in which $15 million dollars had to be cut, leading to school closures, reconstitutions, and other major disruptions. Yet because of the relationships and trust developed, 96% of their teachers approved their contract in the same year and in record time!
- In Pottstown School District, a small district near Philadelphia, Pennsylvania, all seven district schools made AYP in 2009 for the first time in district history. Graduation rates have consistently improved, and time out of the classroom for disruptive behavior has been reduced by 78%.
- A February 2011 report from the American Institutes of Research states that in the 34 schools studied in Mansfield, Texas, Independent School District, "The relationship between implementation [of the process] and [student] achievement was generally strong."

> This report and two other independent studies can be found at www.Hopefoundation.org.

The next section of this chapter provides insight into why PD and networks have been embraced in countries throughout the world—but not as well in the United States. Both the peril and the opportunity this poses are discussed as well as a moral and economic imperative for action. Closing the chapter is a brief summary of what works, what doesn't, and what's next. *The answers are at hand; the question is how will we get people to use them?*

SOME COMMON CORE PRINCIPLES OF NETWORKING AND POSITIVE DEVIANCE

The networking process described in this book was developed separately from PD research and was designed to advance school improvement. PD was initially focused on addressing social ills. It is based on the observation that in every community there are certain individuals or groups (the positive deviants) whose uncommon but successful behaviors or strategies enable these individuals or groups to find a better solution to a problem than their peers, who also face the same challenges and obstacles (Pascale et al., 2010).

The two independent processes share many common features, however. Whether a group is using networks or PD, one key to the success in both is that those using these processes must *want* to change, and they must own both the problem and the solution to it. No level of top-down mandate has succeeded over time in achieving the kind of outcomes that a group committed to its own development has (Pascale et al., 2010). The community must make the discovery itself. In summarizing the thinking of some of the greatest change agents in the world, Peter Block explains that "people will be accountable and committed to what they have a hand in creating . . . whatever the world demands of us, the people most involved have the collective wisdom to meet the requirements of that demand. And if we get them in the room together, in the right context and with a few simple ground rules, the wisdom to create a future or solve a problem is almost always in the room"(Block, 2008, p. xx). Put another way, Dennis Sparks, former Executive Director of Learning Forward, said: "It's pretty easy to divide the world into two categories: one that believes the answer is in the community; and those who think that people in school just don't know enough; they don't even know that they don't know; and they need someone to tell them what to do and make them do it" (D. Sparks, personal communication, 2010).

CHALLENGES TO SCALING SUCCESS IN U.S. EDUCATION

Many reasons exist for this lack of transference of excellent practice within and between U.S. schools. Several will be addressed later in the book. For now, let's consider just two that relate to Sparks's comment:

The General Climate in U.S. Education at This Juncture Is One of Blame and Fear

In response to the above scenario, in which one teacher was convinced that no one in the school was succeeding with certain students, when in fact there were some *outliers* who did perform well with those students, one can almost hear policymakers suggest, "Fire all those other teachers and keep that good one!" This implies a simplistic and erroneous understanding of the problem. As in the case in Vietnam, there are very few *bad guys* in education. None of the parents in Vietnam wanted their children to starve; and no teachers enter the profession to starve their children of an education, either. What was lacking in both cases was a *method* for success and a means to share and scale that method.

Enlightened for-profit corporate leaders would not pursue a path of mass firings of *bad* employees. That is because they are practical bottom-line people, and this is an impractical path to follow—it would not work. Firing large numbers of staff on a regular basis for lack of knowledge, skill, or even motivation would alienate even the high performers, as they would become targets for everyone else. It would cause great internal conflict and upheaval in the organization as staff continually turned over and trust evaporated. Rather than treating everyone poorly for the bad performance of a few people, the corporation would instead develop processes to recruit better, train more effectively, and retain its workforce, using its high-flyers as resources.

Almost everyone among the 50 experts interviewed for this book brought up issues of trust, which is perhaps the most critical element to successful school reform

(Blankstein, 2004/2010; Bryk & Schneider, 2002; Bryk, Sebring, Allensworth, Luppescu, & Easton, 2010). Trust is an ongoing subtheme throughout this book, and the means to create it are provided despite the noxious context in which we are operating.

Cheryl Williams, Executive Director of Learning First Alliance, said: "We are in an unprecedented dangerous spot for public education. There's no one speaking hopefully or supportively of a system that works really hard to do the best job it can under incredibly difficult circumstances. The only popular heroes around public education are those tearing it down" (C. Williams, personal communication, 2010). Phillip Schlechty put it more bluntly: "We are at risk of losing public education." (P. Schlechty, personal communication, 2010). Michelle Norris, award-winning journalist for NPR's *All Things Considered*, said, "If you listen to news you would think U.S. education is under assault. The U.S. education system has to take control of its own story. It is about people getting up every morning committed to our children" (Norris, 2010).

Contrast this thinking to Finland's, which is the number-one ranked Western country in the world according to the rankings on Programme for International Student Assessment (PISA), whose motto is "Trust through Professionalism" (T. Wagner, personal communication, 2010). Not only is this spoken, posted, and understood from the Ministry of Education down, but it is acted on! They recruit their teachers from the top 20% of college graduating classes and pay them accordingly (T. Wagner, personal communication, 2010). Why? Because when the leadership of Finland decided 40 years ago that it was near collapse, it plotted a strategy that put education at the center of its efforts to become a great nation.

Great nations trust their educators and support them. What would the motto for America be in terms of its educational profession? "The flogging will continue until morale improves!"? One can find many reasons not to learn from other educational systems (e.g., Finland is smaller, America is more diverse, and so on). Some of the most conservative and pragmatic entities in the world do just that. For example, Estonia's methods for protecting against cyber attacks are so advanced that the U.S. Pentagon has not only learned from them, but has based its Cyber Defense Excellence Center in Estonia.

The bottom line is this: Successful leaders we have worked with have created trust within their staff and school community, even if trust was totally absent beforehand. Stories with underlying trust subthemes follow in the next chapter and throughout. Yet, as you will read, these courageous individuals did this against the context in which they operated. It's akin to having an enjoyable family picnic while the forest behind you is burning. It's possible but tough, and it takes exceptional focus to pull it off at scale.

Low-Level, High-Stakes Testing Is Sapping Our Energy, Time, and Focus

"We work with some schools where you could almost cry to see them spend a month before exams doing nothing else but taking practice tests" Gene Bottoms, Senior VP, Southern Regional Educational Board (G. Bottoms, personal communication, 2010).

Everyone interviewed for this book concurred on the detrimental effects of basic skills testing as the primary means of gauging our children's success. Even strong advocates for using such testing to at least assure students get basic skills see their limitations. Although extremely successful in his role as New York City Schools Chancellor, Joel Klein, for example, shared that the one thing he would have done differently would have been to provide a richer means of assessing student learning (J. Klein, personal communication, 2010). When questioning students or educators about their number-one complaint regarding school, they will confidently and vociferously sing out this answer in unison: It's boring!

A bifurcation of education exists in this and other lower ranked countries in the world (Knowledge Society, Hargreaves), and the basic *three Rs* curriculum is not what the highest performing schools have traditionally used. Yet, even a growing number of more affluent schools are focusing on AYP and becoming complacent with proficiency instead of pushing further (P. Noguera, personal communication, 2010) toward "closing the global achievement gap" (T. Wagner, personal communication, 2010). In fact, in a world where any child can access the answer to virtually any closed-ended question (e.g., When did the French Revolution begin?), drilling this kind of information as the core of our curriculum is long outdated.

John Wilson, the Executive Director of the National Education Association (NEA), commenting on high-stakes testing said, "I think that people are so frightened by high-stakes tests that they are trying to hold on to the logic that if you teach to the test and practice for tests that you will get better test scores. I think that logic will be proven incorrect" (J. Wilson, personal communication, 2010). Indeed, preliminary research from the Gates Foundation indicates an interesting irony summarized by Vicki Phillips: "The teachers who incessantly drill their students to prepare for standardized tests tend to have lower value-added learning gains than those who simply work their way methodically through the key concepts of literacy and mathematics."

Assuming a higher level curriculum, issues still exist with regard to using more effective assessments. Jay McTighe and Ken O'Connor have long been advocates of performance and observational assessments. Instead of relying on multiple-choice questions and "reinforcing a reductionist view of teaching and learning" (J. McTighe, personal communication, 2010), Canadian education tends to rely on writing, doing, and saying as means of demonstrating knowledge and proficiency (K. O'Connor, personal communication, 2010). But getting breathing room from various forms of test-prep isn't easy to do—especially in lower performing schools that have to show immediate success. According to Phil Schlechty: "Bureaucracy doesn't allow creativity, and you have to be a courageous teacher to teach well in this environment because the results we want are passing low-level tests" (Schlechty, personal communication, 2010).

"In America there is a huge trust problem, which doesn't exist in Finland, Singapore, or Shanghai" (the highest-ranking countries on PISA) (J. Wilson, personal communication, 2010). It's interesting to note that in Finland—always among the top-ranked nations in the world—testing is barely a factor in a student's life. They adhere to the concept that "you can't inspect quality into the product" (Deming, 1982). Instead, quality is part of the front end of the system—in Finland's case, that would include teacher recruitment, financial and professional support, and training as well as the autonomy to make excellent decisions.

Low-level, basic skills' testing not only puts America at a disadvantage internationally compared with countries that emphasize critical thinking, problem-solving, and authentic learning experiences, but it also presents a challenge for scaling PD across a network of schools. This is because the first fundamental axiom for success is that the school community must be the one to define its problem, and external mandates will meet with compliance at best and hunkering down "until this, too, passes" at worst.

Nonetheless, some school leaders and school communities are managing to scale their successes even within this context. Some of these successes will be discussed in the next chapter and beyond.

The remaining portion of this chapter discusses the moral and economic imperative for why we must act on what we know now. The chapter concludes with questions around what is working, what could be next for school communities, and why we can't wait.

THE MORAL AND ECONOMIC IMPERATIVE FOR CHANGE IS NOW

On April 16, 1963, Martin Luther King, Jr., wrote a letter to his fellow clergymen from a jail in Birmingham, Alabama, during one of the many times he was incarcerated to forestall his pursuit of justice and opportunity for *all* Americans, especially those for whom it had been denied, most notably "Negros." His powerful letter included this passage:

> We know through painful experience that freedom is never voluntarily given by the oppressor; it must be demanded by the oppressed. Frankly, I have yet to engage in a direct action campaign that was "well timed" in the view of those who have not suffered unduly from the disease of segregation. For years now I have heard the word "Wait!" It rings in the ear of every Negro with piercing familiarity. This "Wait" has almost always meant "Never." We must come to see, with one of our distinguished jurists, that "justice too long delayed is justice denied." (King, 1963)

Martin Luther King, Jr., was writing this letter to a group of *sympathetic* clergy. In the 1960s, some Americans may have truly wanted a shift in timing or tactics. Others likely preferred the movement to go away all together. Yet, Dr. King was clear on his personal commitment to the cause and the collective exigency of moving forward. What is our individual and collective commitment to the children who need us most? Must the children wait? *The brutal fact is that educational and financial outcomes are inextricably tied—both for individuals and for the nation in which they live.*

For MLK Jr. and an entire people he represented, the time for waiting was over. The stark injustice that had endured for centuries had to end. It was vile and clearly destructive to *everyone* involved, including those perpetuating the system at their own moral, spiritual, and ultimately physical and emotional peril. It was beyond time for a change.

For many, education is the civil rights struggle of the 21st century. The Jim Crow signs are now obfuscated and veiled by a seemingly egalitarian *welcome to all* (if you have the money). And the financial pass necessary to gain everything from access to affordable health care, healthy foods to eat, and a *good education* is disproportionately denied to Hispanic, black, and economically disadvantaged people in the United States (Day & Newburger, 2002). Only about 50% of America's black and Hispanic students graduate high school, compared with more than 85% of their white counterparts. Those who do graduate are destined to receive salaries that are roughly 30% less than their white peers with similar credentials (Day & Newburger). An even bigger economic disparity is between *anyone* who drops out of high school ($1 million average lifetime earnings) versus someone with an advanced degree ($3.4 million for PhD and $4.4 million professional degree) (Day & Newburger). So racism must now share the light with classism, and both are tearing at our moral fiber and slowing America's engine.

The United States ranks in the middle of the pack, sandwiched between Iceland and Lichtenstein, in the PISA rankings on Reading subscales, for example. It is important to note that the countries at the top of the PISA rankings have the lowest variation in students' scores. So although Shanghai has gross domestic product per capita well below the average of countries that participate in the rankings, virtually all of the children there get a good education—poor and rich alike. By contrast, America is well above the mean in terms of the correlation between socioeconomic background of the students tested and their reading performance (PISA, 2009). As the PISA report indicates, the United States falls short of all students getting a *good education*, which is why it ranks relatively low in international standing.

Education is at the epicenter of our equity and economic struggles this century, and the outcome will determine our society as a whole. According to Thomas Friedman (2008), we in America have just *barely* enough time to get back in the race and forestall our dramatic economic slide—but only if we start *immediately.*

A wealthy or even middle-class person reading about the disparities of education (which invariably lead to economic disparities) may feel uncomfortable yet insulated from these statistics. Yet it is interesting to note that the larger the educational gap within a society, the greater the health and social problems for *everyone* in that society—not just for those at the lower rungs (Wilkinson & Pickett, 2009).

WHAT WORKS, WHAT DOESN'T, WHAT'S NEXT?

Success Is at Hand—If We Want It

In Vietnam, the *outsiders* quickly enlisted the insiders—including families who were most impacted by famine, local researchers, and the overall community—to solve their own problem of famine. For this process to work, those receiving the *treatment* have to want it very badly.

The community defines the problem and owns it themselves because, in this process, they also solve the problem. The problem can't be mandated, driven by a competition or a grant. It can't be owned by a grant writer or a distant or local leader. The community with the problem *is* the problem and the solution. They must lead themselves accordingly.

One important early step in Vietnam was for both formal and informal *researchers* to learn how to observe families who were *positive deviants*. Creating a common language and diagnostic was essential.

Having a common language in all schools participating in a network is a big challenge and an early agenda item that never fully goes away. For example, what does *good instruction* mean? What does it look like? How do you improve it? What is student engagement exactly? In any given school on any given day you can get as many answers to these questions as there are staff members. Getting common language and clarity around such matters are critical to success, and a process and framework for doing so is included in Chapter 5.

At a certain point, the researchers in Vietnam knew the answer. They had observed enough families to see that those who were well-nourished did things that others did not—such as adding to their meals small shrimp or crabs they found while working in the rice paddies, feeding their children four to five times a day to accommodate their small stomachs versus the normal two times a day, and using better hygiene. This was the *what*—the technical side of the equation that Pascale and colleagues call "the easy part—and only 20% of the work. What matters far more is the *how*—the very particular journey that each community must engage in to mobilize itself, overcome resignation and fatalism, discover its latent wisdom, and put this wisdom into practice. This bears repeating: *The community must make the discovery itself.* It alone determines how change can be disseminated through the *practice* of new behavior—not through explanation or edict" (Pascale, et al., 2010, p. x).

Similarly, school leadership teams that become engaged in districtwide networks learn to become like researchers. They often begin by saying: "We already do that!" (The subtext being: "I'm already doing a good job. Why do I have to do this?") Through processes described throughout this book, trust is built, egos fade, and new relationships form, providing the additional motivation to truly *learn* together with the entire community. All this presumes a courageous leader as described in Chapter 3—one who is strong enough *not* to always take charge and instead to trust the process and the people to define and solve their own problem.

As in the example of what happened in Vietnam, likewise, members of the leadership team begin learning what they need to know to succeed. And as in the case of the Vietnamese researchers, they then have a new challenge: How to get everyone *else* to know what they know and to *act* on it. Likewise, how do we keep everyone *engaged* in the process when there is so much potential for some to see themselves as excluded from the *inner* circle?

These are but many of the social challenges that arise in networking schools, or spreading PD. Many more exist—even beginning with a clear distinction between, for example, the PD approach which necessitates ownership and derives answers from the inside, and *best practices,* which are often imported from elsewhere.

THE BIG QUESTION

So often the question *is* the answer. As in the Vietnam case, we have come to a point where we have many of the answers. We know what works in so many instances. We know how to find and scale excellence within an entire district and even across districts. Knowing *what* is the easy part. Knowing *how* must always, by definition of this process, involve those who will use that *what,* be affected by it, want to have it, own it, and grow it. So herein lies the question for you the reader: What will it take for you and your community to use a process that can scale what is already working within your school(s) and, as a part of that process, build your leadership capacity to sustain and enhance those successes?

The next chapter will more fully describe this sustainable process in scaling student success. The question remains, however, what will you do with it? As you go through and think about this, feel free to access a community of your peers at Answerisintheroom.org, who are doing the same thing and grappling with the same questions at www.answerisin theroom.org. Time is short. The answers are at hand. Lives are at stake. The world is in our hands. That's why we can't wait.

A Process to CREATE Sustained Student Success

"People don't have a language to talk about teaching and learning."

—Richard Elmore

"He who has a strong enough 'why' can bear almost any 'how.'"

—Friedrich Nietzsche, German philosopher (1844–1900)

A MOVEMENT IS BORN IN U.S. EDUCATION—AND EXPORTED TO OTHER NATIONS

On February 3, 1989, quality guru W. Edwards Deming joined a group of leaders in education for the first time to share the principles he had shared with the Japanese after World War II. At that time, General Douglas MacArthur asked Deming to be a part of the Marshall Plan to help rebuild Japan. More than 20 CEOs from the largest corporations such as Toyota and Sony gathered to hear about the management and leadership practices that had led to making such a powerful and triumphant country (Deming, 1982). Deming said, in effect, that he would share something better than what is being used in the United States—something America was unwilling to listen to for decades—a new brand of management. It included revolutionary principles such as #1: Constancy of Purpose and #8: Drive Out Fear in the Organization—principles that were based on what *really* motivates people, not carrots and sticks (Pink, 2009).

Decades later, Deming continued to share that same message, but now with educational leaders, CEOs, and governors in a series of HOPE Foundation Shaping America's Future forums. Domestically, this in turn led directly to the publication of seminal works by DuFour and Eaker on professional learning communities by the conveners of these forums and later

HOPE's use of *networking* via a process that could be replicated in virtually any setting to find and scale what is already working within a school or district. That work began in Alton, Illinois, in 2000 and quickly included schools in Milwaukee, and Newport News, Virginia, where the HOPE Foundation supported the creation and implementation of what their superintendent at that time, Marcus Newsome, and leadership team termed a "paired school" model.

The method of schools helping schools and the strong helping the weak that was first pioneered in Newport News was eventually evaluated by Andy Hargreaves and Dennis Shirley (2009) in a network of 300 underperforming schools connected to and supported by stronger partners with similar students. This principle of schools helping schools rather than undergoing repeated interventions from above became a cornerstone of their fourth way of educational reform that replaced the first way of unregulated innovation in the 1970s, the use of competition, force, and standardization in the second way, and the obsession with data and spreadsheets as providing all the answers in the third way.

As Andy Hargreaves indicated at the Learning Forward conference in December 2010, this was the first effort in the United States in which lower and higher performing schools became responsible for one another's performance. In a prior conversation, Hargreaves shared that this concept spread from Virginia to Bristol, England, through Alan Boyle who spearheaded what was soon after supported throughout the United Kingdom (Hargreaves, 2010). The concept is popularly known as "networking" schools, both in the United Kingdom and Canada.

Meanwhile, in the United States, the idea of using a process throughout the district—such as one for spreading positive deviance, or systematically building a common language and capacity using principles such as those found in *Failure Is Not an Option®: 6 Principles That Guide Student Achievement in High-Performing Schools*—is far from the norm (Blankstein, 2004/2010).

Figure 2.1 *Failure Is Not an Option®: 6 Principles*

1. Common mission, vision, values, and goals

2. Achievement for all students through prevention and intervention systems

3. Collaborative teaming focused on teaching for learning

4. Data-based decisions for continuous improvement

5. Active family and community engagement

6. Building sustainable leadership capacity

Few district leaders in the United States have been prepared to focus on a workable process for scaling excellence throughout the system in a manner described in this book. Some reasons for this are shared in the prior and next chapters. Yet this process is in fact underway in very diverse settings to the betterment of their children and staff.

THE CATALYST TO CHANGE

The precursor to this process, or any *sustainable* improvement, is an urgent need to change identified by the school *community* itself. That community must define a problem it wants very much to solve. As with all other parts of the process, this problem cannot be defined or mandated by an external source; however, it could be catalyzed or facilitated externally.

The McKinsey/OECD (2010) report, for example, indicates that the two common external catalysts for change in countries "on the move" are either a crisis or an external report (presumably creating some kind of internal crisis or debate). Domestically, the parallel might be a school that is being threatened with closure. Yet even when the need to change is fully recognized internally, this alone does not assure success. More often the reason for failure in the first place is a lack of collective capacity rather than lack of will or desire. The desire is simply the important first step to sustainable improvement, but too often the community is simply stuck and doesn't know how to proceed. The methodology described below is meant to address this.

In addition to the two catalysts for change mentioned above, we have fortunately found a third as well: inspiration or desire to do even better by all children. Although *successful* school districts are sometimes in reality cruising, or on autopilot, there are others that are inspired to do better by a deeply committed leader and/or lead team. Mansfield Independent School District outside of Dallas, Texas, is one such district that went from good to great without any external requirements to do so. Some of the reasons surrounding its success are shared in the following chapters.

THE CREATE PROCESS

Regardless of which of the three catalysts mentioned previously starts the process, the best method we know of to create the needed change is, for the purposes of this book, named CREATE. This process allows a school community to effectively spread what is already working within its own walls to all parts of the school or district. This process that we have used explicitly and have seen develop organically over time is outlined in detail as follows:

Commitment is made by leadership to a new vision and process for change, and both are made clear to the community (more in Chapter 3—"The Courage to Commit to the Work").

Resources are committed and team(s) formed to tackle the problem and improve outcomes. The most important of these resources are *not* financial (see Chapter 4).

Excellence as clearly defined by the teams along with a common language and framework for action (*) to use within the schools (excellence will be discussed in Chapter 5).

Action planning to collect and share what is already working is collectively agreed upon (see Chapter 6).

Transference of knowledge with the larger school community around the work deepens and broadens the learning, relations, and commitment (more on transference will be addressed in Chapter 7).

Embedding new learning in the school culture through routines, rituals, and alignment is the foundation for sustainability (see Chapter 8).

(*) The six principles in *Failure Is Not an Option* comprise the framework used in this book, but others could be used as well. Deming's 14 principles and the Framework of Essential Supports (Bryk et al., 2010) are excellent examples.

Effective frameworks are open-ended and allow for great flexibility in determining strategy, content, and curriculum. (See how Williamston Middle School brought in various curricular approaches with one framework, Chapter 6.)

The two case stories following demonstrate how this process plays out in very different contexts. The first case is about a preK–5 elementary school in Brooklyn, New York, that was on the verge of being closed down. Their approach to the work required them to take additional steps (such as simply bringing order to the school), as their situation was dire. They also used *Failure Is Not An Option®* and supportive training as a foundation but did the rest of the work on their own.

The second case is in Fort Wayne, Indiana, which has 51 schools, including elementary, intermediate (1–8), middle, and high school(s). Although they share many of the same urban demographics with the New York school, they had far more resources, more complexity, and more than 50 schools. They also planned for a comprehensive effort to bring about cohesion and excellence systemwide.

Case Story 1:
Jackie Robinson Elementary School: A School in Crisis

Marion Wilson was hired May 31, 2006, as the sixth principal in 5 years to run Jackie Robinson, an elementary school in Brooklyn, New York. However, because of the extensive protests underway outside and inside the school, she couldn't go to work for an entire week. Waiting instead at the district office, she drafted a mission and vision for the school that she knew she would never be able to unveil. She also knew she would instead need to cocreate a mission and primary focus that everyone could agree upon. She acted on her own commitment by using that week to memorize school personnel's names and information on their backgrounds to help her win over the hostile staff.

On June 6, 2006, the Superintendent held a meeting with staff in the auditorium to introduce Ms. Wilson. During the meeting, the district union leader stood and said: "No disrespect to you, but we don't want you here. We want the principal who was here before you," and she walked out. One by one each teacher walked out of the auditorium. Marion didn't know what to do.

That week she began to tour the school and found many doors had been locked to keep her out. When she did enter a classroom, she found kids sitting in rows, and everyone doing their own thing; none of them would even acknowledge her. A fifth-grade teacher didn't answer Ms. Wilson's "Hello" on three occasions. Ms. Wilson said, "Isn't your name Ms. Thomas? Do I know you? Do you know me?

I talked to you three times, and you haven't answered me." The woman replied: "Nothing personal, but I want the principal who was here before you to come back." Ms. Wilson explained: "You may not like me, but you need to at least respect me by saying 'Hello.'" The 20 days between June 6 and June 26 when school let out "were the worst days of my life," reported Ms. Wilson.

Her predecessor had been kind and gentle but allowed anything to happen—there were fights, kids walking around aimlessly, and no consistency in instruction. The annual tests revealed failure for the school because of not only scores but also the participation rate, which had to be at least 95% (only 89% of students had even shown up to take the test the January before she arrived).

Being the latest of a string of departing principals, Ms. Wilson decided she needed to do something different. That summer she formed a very small cabinet of four people in the school she trusted, and they planned a retreat that would involve the entire school. The budget office refused to provide the money she would need, but she insisted and prevailed. No one had ever taken the staff out and rarely bought them a book. She needed a way to get everyone cohesive and on board quickly; she used the professional development reform book as the foundation for doing this, and ordered copies for each staff member. She began by forming jigsaw teams at the retreat that coupled stronger and weaker staff, including support personnel and paraprofessionals.

She assured them that moving forward, everything would be based on the six principles in that book, and they created the motto: "Excellence Is the Only Option." This tied in with the book and became their collective vision for every student.

Once back at school, Ms. Wilson's next job was bringing order. She painted a line down the middle of the hallway to direct traffic flow. She also put in place other simple procedures such as creating an orderly dismissal process to prevent all of the kids from running chaotically for the door and into the street to board a bus at the end of the day.

In the first year, she did not address instructional strategies, but she and her cabinet did create a consistent curriculum and processes demonstrating how to use class time more effectively. Ms. Wilson also expanded her team to include supporters as well as many who were on the fence prior. The same teacher who once would not greet her had the courage and the humility to later become among Ms. Wilson's most ardent supporters once trust was established. This teacher, in turn, courageously recruited others to become positive advocates as well.

Together the teachers identified literacy as a focal point for improving all aspects of student learning. In particular, they made a data-based decision to put more emphasis on writing as a high-leverage strategy to fully engage students and enhance overall literacy.

Instructional improvements began with nonthreatening, informal walk-throughs done by her cabinet. They started buddying teachers with one another through initiatives such as *lunch and learn*. Consultants were also brought in, and workshops were held for teachers at locations off campus as a way of building not only skills but affinity for one another and for the new principal who did things differently.

(Continued)

(Continued)

Some of the teachers already knew what was required to provide good instruction and were willing to work hard. She used these teachers to demonstrate good instruction to those who had gone along with the previous culture and had done little. Although the approach to defining good instruction varied, the staff were able to create consistency in curriculum and teaching techniques across all grade levels. This was done by starting with the basics and concentrating on things such as use of time, which was slowly building up to more advanced instructional techniques. The previous model of "let me just talk, hand out dittos, and if the students don't get it, it's their own fault" was steadily erased from the culture.

Eventually the methods used to share good instruction led to friendly gatherings and even friendly competition. For example, all of the third-grade teachers would get together at lunch to plan a lesson, which then inspired the fourth-grade team to do that plus meet again on their own time an additional day. They began to post a teacher of the month as rated by peers, as part of a $50 competition created among the teachers with guidance from the Assistant Principal Mingo, who also personally contributed the prize money. It was based on their attendance, success in the classroom, the assistance they would give to other teachers, and other criteria they codeveloped. Every month the winner was announced at a staff meeting, and everyone applauded and enjoyed the celebration. They also used the bulletin board to publicly post photos and extensive bios and interests of each teacher to give everyone a chance to learn more about one another.

Below is an analysis of the Jackie Robinson Case Story using the CREATE process:

Commitment—The catalyst for change in the case was stark, and in this case it was both external (eminent school closure, a new determined principal) and internal (many were in despair but wanted something better). The principal clearly had the courage to commit to engaging staff around a new vision for the school and the students it would serve, and that enabled her to endure the worst 20 days of her life and much more to follow.

Resources—The resources she committed to the change effort were primarily her time and that of her cabinet, yet they also included more tangible resources than that community had experienced in their time together. The retreat was meant as a demonstration of a new day, and the books were used to illuminate the path they would now travel.

Excellence—The time they took to jigsaw, discuss, iterate, go to workshops, and begin that process of discussion and iteration anew was all designed to create the common language around what *excellence* meant. The six principles served as their framework for action and means of developing cohesive actions.

Action Planning—The weekly lunch and learns and other small team gatherings were designed to share what was working and decide how to disseminate that more widely throughout the building via their monthly meetings and summer retreat. In so doing, they deepened their learning and relations across the school community. By publicly sharing what they were doing and what was working and mutually agreeing to next steps, they also deepened their commitment to further action.

Transference—The learning walks and weekly meetings were designed to share what was working and bring it to scale. The friendly gatherings and informal competitions around putting in extra time to meet and learn from one another further expedited transference of skills and knowledge.

Embedding—Through competitions such as the teacher of the month as selected by peers and based on criteria that align with the mission, vision, values, and goals of the school (such as cooperation with peers, continuous improvement, and so on), the school has begun to embed the desired changes in the culture. There are many more such rituals and routines. Their data walls are large and publicly displayed in the hallways for all to see. The prior lack of trust would never have allowed for that. Student engagement is rich and involves the arts, sciences, and the community. It is typified by a daily poem created and recited by students that roots them in the valiant history of Jackie Robinson and ends in "Success Is Our ONLY Option!"

Figure 2.2   The CREATE Process

Case Story 2:
Fort Wayne Community Schools Scale Up
Success Throughout the District

Fort Wayne Community Schools (FWCS) Superintendent Dr. Wendy Robinson and her team decided to move forward with the systemwide implementation seeing the CREATE process work on a smaller scale. It began with Carolyn Powers, now one of two elementary directors for FWCS. She was an elementary principal in 2005 when she began the journey. Like Ms. Wilson, it began with reading a book and attending related conferences. Ms. Powers then saw her own school's performance improved and discussed expanding the process to other schools with Dan Bickel, the Elementary Area Administrator who oversees all elementary schools. Mr. Bickel, who also believed that the CREATE process had value, took the idea to Superintendent Dr. Robinson. The district's administrative team decided to pilot with six elementary schools the CREATE process described previously through what is known as the Courageous Leadership Academy. Based on the outcomes of the 2008–2009 first year for the six schools (typified by Shambaugh's results following), the district leadership decided to go systemwide, and they engaged all 53 of their schools in the academic year 2009–2010. (Now there are 51 schools because of closing an elementary and a high school due to budget reductions.)

Figure 2.3 Percentages of Students Reading at Grade Level at Shambaugh Elementary School

Grade	Quarter 1	Quarter 4
Kindergarten	51%	97%
First	80%	84%
Second	46%	67%
Third	61%	75%
Fourth	48%	63%
Fifth	48%	70%

Reprinted with permission.

Source: S. Smiley, N. Noel, S. Lothamer, C. Rasor, D. Pelkington, C. Kobi-Berger, L. Beer, M. Bestard, and D. Hyatt; personal communication; 2009.

The outcomes in the 2009–2010 school year have been substantial gains across the board for all participating schools in terms of overall achievement, closing gaps between subgroups, and comparison achievement with the state (see Figure 2.4 for complete set of statistics). There are 79 languages spoken in the FWCS district, and 68% of their students are on free or reduced-price lunch.

In addition, FWCS is one of the few districts in the country that has to make progress in all 37 subgroups of students in order to make adequate yearly progress, and it did that for the first time in its history in 2010. (Of some 15,000 districts in the United States, only 70 are required to progress in all 37 subgroups.)

According to Powers, the district has come together and really jelled over the past few years—even in the case of extreme adversity. In early 2010, for example, 11 schools were identified as potential targets to be further scrutinized by the state. Superintendent Robinson and her team preempted that by reconstituting them. All staff had to reapply for their jobs. Interview questions and a rubric to determine the strength of the candidate's answer became identical throughout the district, based, in part, on the common framework of the six principles as well as a newly written teacher job description. It was extremely important that teachers understand the requirements of the job before applying and entering into an interview. The demands on our teachers in our LEAD schools and throughout the district have evolved, with a new understanding of data and instruction at the core of their job. Teachers were hired with no weight given to seniority, a monumental shift from hiring procedures nationwide. Dr. Robinson made explicit the commitment to that level of cohesion, reiterated by the need to follow the rubric to ensure the right teachers were hired for each building team This restructuring was accompanied by a $15 million budget cut, yet because of the common language and commitments that had been developed, 96% of the teachers approved their contract for the coming year.

The entire district has come together around instruction as well. Common rubrics, for example, have been jointly created to assess student work, so there is a common understanding of excellence. Powers said levels are working together in unprecedented ways after realizing that their challenges are similar. She recounted one high school principal saying the levels "are not that different after all."

The Fort Wayne Community Schools case story above is an overview of some of the outcomes of the CREATE process the district underwent in their Courageous Leadership Academies (CLA). Below is an analysis of this school district using the CREATE process as a backdrop:

Figure 2.4   Fort Wayne Community Schools (FWCS) Achievement Outcomes, 2009 v. 2010

Grade	English Language Arts			Math		
	Spring 2009 ISTEP	Acuity Predictive B*	Spring 2010 ISTEP	Spring 2009 ISTEP	Acuity Predictive B*	Spring 2010 ISTEP
3	64	73	73	60	66	66
4	64	69	70	60	66	65
5	61	68	66	70	75	74
6	53	65	63	61	62	67
7	52	60	59	55	55	61
8	51	57	58	56	54	64

*Acuity Assessments are diagnostic assessments aligned to Indiana's Academic Standards.

ISTEP 2010: FWCS v. Indiana—Percent Passing E/la						
	FWCS			Indiana		
Grade	Spring 2009	Spring 2010	Change	Spring 2009	Spring 2010	Change
3	64	73	9	74	79	5
4	64	70	6	73	77	4
5	61	66	5	70	71	1
6	53	60	7	69	72	3
7	52	59	7	67	72	5
8	51	54	3	65	69	4

ISTEP 2010: FWCS v. Indiana—Percent Passing Mathematics						
	FWCS			Indiana		
Grade	Spring 2009	Spring 2010	Change	Spring 2009	Spring 2010	Change
3	60	66	6	72	75	3
4	60	65	5	70	75	5
5	70	74	4	76	80	4
6	61	65	4	73	77	4
7	55	61	6	69	73	4
8	56	60	4	67	72	5

FWCS ISTEP + Results 2009 vs. 2010						
	English/Language Arts			Mathematics		
Grade	Spring 2009 ISTEP	Spring 2010 ISTEP	Change	Spring 2009 ISTEP	Spring 2010 ISTEP	Change
3	64	74	10+	60	67	7+
4	64	70	6+	60	66	6+
5	61	67	6+	70	75	5+
6	53	63	10+	61	67	6+
7	52	60	8+	55	62	7+
8	51	58	7+	56	64	8+

Note: Spring 2010 scores reflect final results as of August 2010.

Commitment—Once the district decided to expand the experience beyond the six elementary schools, the leader and her team committed considerable political and human capital to achieving excellence across the district.

Resources—This led a steering committee at the district level to use the six principles of *Failure Is Not an Option*® as a framework to guide their decision about the most pressing area they wanted to address first. A steering committee in a districtwide, regional, or provincial network is essential.

Excellence—Since the six principles act as a system and are not independent of one another (see Figure 2.1 page 14), any one of them can be an entry point that will eventually involve all others as well.

An early focus was one of developing a common definition and rubric around what good instruction looked like (Principle #3, Figure 2.1). Further, to build sustainable leadership capacity (Principle #6) they developed a common questionnaire and scoring for prospective new personnel.

Action Planning—Leadership teams were invited to several CLA cohorts in order to keep each small enough for extensive interaction needed to build relations and develop coherence. At the end of each cohort meeting (there were four each year), the leadership teams determined their "reentry plan" so as to engage the rest of their learning communities.

Transference—Teams practiced what they had learned within the academy and received structured peer feedback. They committed within their teams, across teams, to their district and to the external facilitating organization to go back to their schools and use the tools they had developed and/or utilized together during their CLA session, and then bring back artifacts to their next session representing what's working.

Embedding—The next session would orchestrate sharing across teams using specific protocols that became standard so as to build the trust and open communication while maintaining the rigor of conversation.

These working sessions served the purpose of learning across the district while normalizing practice. The sharing-out portion of these sessions built greater trust, and a more extensive network of colleagues to whom each team member could go for advice, new strategies, and support. The pronouncements of next steps as well as what was already working served to create lateral accountability and to deepen commitment to action across the entire learning community. Processes learned and practiced in the academy were recreated at the school level and the repetition provided one pillar for embedding them (see Chapter 8 on "Embedding the New Learning in the Culture for Sustainability" for the "Three Pillars of Embedding the Process in the School Culture").

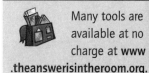 Many tools are available at no charge at **www .theanswerisintheroom.org.**

THE ADVANTAGES OF THE CREATE PROCESS

Although the two case studies in this chapter—and the many other places in which this process is undertaken—vary widely in demography, resources, and developmental stage, they meet with similarly impressive results. Those results go well beyond short-term gains judged by students' test scores. They include a robust leadership team that has the capacity to continuously improve, and the tools, language, process, and commitment necessary to handle extraordinary challenges.

CREATE Versus Traditional Reform Approaches

It is helpful to juxtapose this method against the norm for better clarity around the differences between the two.

Figure 2.5   Traditional Reform Approaches Compared With the CREATE Process

Traditional Process	CREATE Process
Leader decides direction	Leader facilitates school community decisions, and becomes a learner as well
Leader gets "*buy-in*" to a predetermined outcome	Questions & analysis lead to discoveries that drive collective, focused action
Those who don't buy in are "resisters"	Process leads to collective commitment
Focus on programs and people getting outcomes	Focus on scaling specific, high-leverage behaviors that yield desired results
Programs, experts, structures are imported	The answer is already in the room—capacity is built to identify and scale those answers
High costs for external expertise	Low costs for internal expertise
Sustainability not addressed, or if so, only after launch	Sustainability built into day one by virtue of gaining depth and breadth of engagement

THE BIG QUESTION

The big question for you, the reader, is: What compelling problem or challenge does your community face that could be a catalyst for you to undertake a focused, concerted process such as this? You can join colleagues in working through this answer at www.answerisin theroom.org.

The next chapter provides insights into the kind of leadership needed to successfully sail in these waters.

The Courage to Commit to the Work

"Courage is the Mother of all virtues because without it, you cannot consistently perform all the others."

—Aristotle

"Leaders who wish to shape the school culture change themselves first."

—Dennis Sparks

Throughout the ages, across geographies, ethnicities, religions, and cultures, *courage* has been consistently deemed the number-one virtue (Blankstein, 2004/2010). Consider this small sampling:

> *Without Courage, all other virtues lose their meaning. Courage is, rightly esteemed, the first of human qualities, because . . . it is the quality that guarantees all others.*—Sir Winston Churchill
>
> *The ultimate measure of a man is not where he stands in moments of comfort, but where he stands at times of challenge and controversy. Courage faces fear and thereby masters it; cowardice represses fear and is thereby mastered by it. We must build dikes of courage to hold back the flood of fear.*—Martin Luther King, Jr.
>
> *Courage may be the most important of all virtues, because without it one cannot practice any other virtue with consistency.*—Maya Angelou
>
> *Courage, the footstool of the virtues, upon which they stand.*—Robert Louis Stevenson

But what exactly is courage and where does it come from? Can it be developed? How are courage and commitment linked to leadership? Are both necessary to succeed in leading today's schools? This chapter will flesh out these questions and share examples of how courage and commitment play themselves out in education. The focus will then turn to building one's individual and collective capacity for courageous actions and commitments. Finally, tools on how to enlarge your courageous community will be explored. This chapter will also ask you to courageously reflect on your experiences. Let's begin first with a clear and common definition of courage.

DEFINING COURAGE

> *"Undertaking the new process requires the courage to have conviction without answers and the openness to learn together"* (Senge, 2006, p. x).

The above reference to courage aligns with one found in *John Dewey's Ethical Democracy as Experience* (Pappas, 2008) in which the author identifies courage as being open-minded, listening to others, and opening oneself to difference ways of thinking of things while also sticking up for your pre-existing beliefs. This would indeed be courageous, from the standpoint of this book, were it also to require the person to overcome fear and take all that on for a greater good.

In the original version of *Failure Is Not an Option,* Chapter 2 is dedicated to courageous leadership and harkens back to the origins and early uses of the concept of courage (Blankstein, 2004). Briefly, courage comes from the French root "le Coeur," or "the heart." For Native Americans, such as the Lakota Sioux, courage was something to be developed among young "Braves" (Eastman, 1902). Courage involves sacrifice on behalf of the greater good, and for the Lakota Sioux, there were rituals that strengthened that virtue. Although the sacrifice might one day be that of one's own life, the idea of dying in battle or saving's someone's life was an extreme depiction of *courage* for the tribe. Yet in modern times, courage has often been equated with life-risking or death-defying activities.

To reclaim courage, this *mother of all virtues,* we also need to reframe it. Taking a cue from ancient societies as well as modern practical applications, "5 Axioms of Courage" were created (Blankstein 2004/2010) and are listed below. The first of them, Begin With Your Core, is revisited and expanded upon in the "3 Commitments of Leadership" section later in this chapter.

Figure 3.1   The 5 Axioms of Courage

1. Begin With Your Core
2. Create Organizational Meaning
3. Maintain Consistency and Clarity of Purpose
4. Confront the Data and Your Fears
5. Build Sustainable Relationships

For the purposes of this book, "courage" is defined as *overcoming fear to act in concert with one's deeply held values on behalf of another person or greater good.* Consider this example:

> A teacher prepared to present to her peers a new technique for differentiating instruction. It was very effective for her in reaching some otherwise disengaged students. Her hands were cold and sweating and there was a lump in her throat. She hadn't slept well, as she worried about how her peers would react. But the principal and those on her team were desperate to help the rest of the staff enhance their skills so that all of the students would succeed. They had prevailed upon her to share what she knew. It was now "show time"!

Although less dramatic than most acts considered to be courageous, the teacher was clearly afraid of the pending challenge. Yet, the teacher did it anyway for the overall good of the staff and students. In this way, it meets the definition above. Had she not had a fear of speaking in front of her peers, or had she done it for self-glorification, it would not have been a courageous act.

In modern day society, most likely we will not perish in battle, but we can save the lives of others—our students. It often will take courage, and rarely is saving students easy. Yet, new and veteran leaders may need to re-commit to be courageous for their students simply to hold to doing what's right in the face of shifting political and economic winds and whims.

With more clarity around what is courage, this "mother of all virtues," we can better determine in what contexts it matters, how to develop courage in the community, and who actually needs to have it to enhance the likelihood of success.

Who Needs Courage?

It's true that it is not essential that everyone in the learning community be courageous for student success to be achieved. The average leader can get by without courage on most days. Yet, the more dynamic, challenging, or complex the environment, the more likely those in the community will have to call upon courage to *do what's right*. That may mean deprivatizing one's teaching practice to expedite learning in the community, telling a *bully* peer that she is not adhering to the new meeting protocols, or admitting to peers that you, the principal or superintendent, "don't know" during a professional learning experience. (For administrators who are female, Lambert and Gardner [2009] argue that women have a more difficult time being courageous because of their socialization of needing to please and avoid conflict.)

Saying you "don't know" and being willing to learn alongside the rest of the staff does not require courage if playing the role comes easily and naturally. For many, however, the process of being a team *learner* will indeed demand much more humility and possibly courage than has traditionally been called for in the running of a school.

As Richard Elmore explained regarding a similar process of *networking* schools that he is endeavoring, "Applying the new practice requires leaders to take risks. They demonstrate vulnerability when receiving support from others who know the process" (R. Elmore, personal communication, December 2010).

In a high-performing school or district, it's often the case that being vulnerable or confronting the data and one's fears (the fourth axiom of courage—Blankstein, 2004/2010) is not part of the culture. These communities often coast in the "land of nice" (R. Elmore, personal communication, December 2010) until forced to change by either new leadership or a new student body that is not "responding to treatment." Although courage may be needed to change these cultures, it is often not called upon in order to get along.

By contrast, in less stable school environments, facing myriad complexities and real conflicts requires a great deal of courage. Think of what it took of Principal Marion Wilson from our last chapter to be the only principal to last more than a school year!

The critical lesson about courage, leadership, and scaling positive deviance through networking is that dramatically different outcomes are now possible within any school district. Achieving them will take a different approach. A different approach will require a different type of leadership and *learnership* than has been the norm. If this sophisticated leadership involved in *letting go*, trusting the process, and being an active participant in learning is also scary, then courage will be required!

 There is a quick self-assessment tool developed by Louise Stoll to gauge the type of school you are working in at **www.theanswerisintheroom .org.**

Consider this response from the HOPE Foundation Honorary Chair and Nobel Peace Prize Laureate Archbishop Desmond Tutu when asked if there was a defining moment for him in which he knew there was total commitment and no turning back:

COURAGEOUS COMMITMENTS

During apartheid, the apartheid government was obsessed with turning South Africa into a haven for whites. But this was hindered by an awkward fact: blacks outnumbered whites 5 to 1.

With cunning the government decided to parcel out South Africa according to ethnicities. The whites, though only 20% of the population, were allocated 87% of the most arable land while the blacks, forming 80% of the population, got only 13%. South Africa's population had, however, mixed together over several decades to occupy the same land and to separate them was like trying to unscramble an omelette. The government designated certain parts of the country as black spots. Populations where blacks were living were eradicated. Homes were demolished and blacks were trucked to poverty-stricken areas to live, often only in shacks. I once visited such a resettlement camp. A little girl lived in a shack with her widowed mother and sister. I asked "Do you have any food?" And she said "We borrow food." Have you returned any of the food you borrowed?" "No."

"What do you do when you can't borrow food?"

"We drink water to fill our stomachs."

These children were not going hungry because there was no food. South Africa was a net exporter of food. No, they were starving by deliberate government policy.

Before this moment I had already been opposed to apartheid, but that incident made me decide to call for sanctions; I said I would tell her story until apartheid was overthrown.

Archbishop Desmond Tutu's unwavering commitment is clear and starkly defined. How did his clarity of commitment connect to the ultimate success he envisioned?

Beginning With Your Core

For the purpose of this book, beginning with the core does not involve yoga or an apple. "The core is defined here as the intersection of one's purpose, values, and intention. Determining one's core is a profound and intensive process that provides the enduring roots necessary to sustain efforts in the face of opposing forces" (Blankstein 2004/2010, p. xx). In *Failure Is Not an Option,* there is a comprehensive section committed to helping the reader develop his core, including these questions:

1. What do I *value* most? Another way to ask this might be, what behaviors can I *not* tolerate?

2. What do my past life patterns, strong interests, and passions tell me about my *purpose* in life?

3. How does that purpose overlap with what I am doing *here* in my current role? What are the *intentions* relative to the work I am now doing? (Blankstein, 2010, p. 39)

Other good questions to consider include: Why did I get into this profession? What do I want my legacy to be?

Effective leaders must always clarify the commitments they are willing to make to themselves. "Authentic leaders build their practice inward from their core commitments rather than outward from a management text" (Evans, 1996, p. x). Furthermore, members within the community must share what commitments they are willing to make to one another.

Another way to look at it is this: What are you, as a school leader and as an individual, willing to *commit* to and to what extent does that commitment go? For example, if the school mission includes "All children will succeed," would that mean that if truancy is an issue, the school puts in place a structure to actively identify and compassionately recruit truants back into the school the same day, as is being done in Baltimore schools. Are teachers willing to meet parents at their homes, or is the school ready to provide transportation to the school when parents lack it? Is there a way for students who start off the semester poorly to recover credits or have initially poor work not factor into their overall grade? Most importantly, is the community willing to commit resources to a process of jointly defining excellence, deprivatizing practice in order to find it, and collectively share what is working? Finally, will the community commit across the district to new practices based on what has been discovered? Pointedly, what can *you* begin doing *today* to help scale student success?

The answer to the above questions and so many more begins with the core commitments of the leader of the district and then the leader of the school. It may take a great deal of courage to even define these commitments for many reasons, yet understanding and then clearly communicating the commitments is critical for long-term success. Christie Alfred, Principal of Ben Barber Career and Technology Academy/Frontier High School in Mansfield Independent School District, put it this way: "I would always communicate with them that I would never ask them to do anything that I wouldn't do or wasn't willing to do *with* them. This helped to build trust."

As explained in the prior chapter, making public statements about personal commitments to action reinforces the likelihood of following through on those actions while it strengthens the resolve of the entire community. Emotions are contagious. So is a bias for action.

A PILLAR OF COURAGE

When a leader knows what he stands for, proclaims it, and then acts on it, momentum is created for others to do the same. This defines commitment. Making mutual commitments is an age-old ritual used in marriage or taking an oath for public office because it is a pillar of success. Everything else is built upon those commitments. Courage often enters into those commitments, especially when the commitments call for facing the unknown. Thoughts such as "How will we achieve this?" and "Can we really do that?" sometimes have no apparent answers, but courageous leaders move forward nonetheless.

Three Keys of Commitments

For the administrator to be steadfast in her commitment, three factors have to be in place for optimal success. (1) The first commitment to be made is internal: from the leader *to* the leader. When making the commitment known to the larger community, it is best to frame it in terms of the personal connection to the larger vision. Saying *I am committed to doing everything in my power to succeed with every single child in this community* is better than saying *I am committed to making sure that* you *succeed with every child!* It is also good to limit the number of commitments. Like with goals, having 36 is like having none—they simply won't be accomplished. Core commitments are few in number. (2) The second commitment is to bringing the new community-created vision in to focus. A distinction should be made between what a leader's core commitments are and what the commitments of the larger school community are going to be. They will surely overlap, but likely not be identical. Although the principal may be willing to work 12 hours a day, for example, that may not be so for every staff member. (3) The third and final commitment centers on making that vision to the commitment a reality. This book describes an inside-out process for engaging the rest of the community.

BUILDING A COLLECTIVE COMMITMENT TO SCALE UP STUDENT SUCCESS

In the first chapter, it was stated that the community *with* the problem *is* the problem *and* the solution. The role of the formal and informal leaders of that community, therefore, is to help identify the challenge starting with what is happening *now* in terms of not only outcomes, but also their practice and the people involved with each.

A team is formed soon thereafter to define and later address the key challenges. A vision is created collectively with the entire community along with SMART goals (the

In the *Tools to Help Answer the Questions in the Room* section in the back of this book, resources for "Writing an Instructional SMART Goal Worksheet" are shown in Tool A and a list of "Strategies for Making Time" is included in Tool B.

milestones along the way to the vision) and values (how we will behave while moving toward that vision), and all of this is tied to the mission (why do we exist as an organization?) (Blankstein, *Failure Is Not an Option*, 2004/2010).

The process by which all the above is endeavored will determine the outcome. *The process is the strategy.* The winning approach is one that will engage and lead to commitment from virtually the entire learning community. Schools that have a vision that they are deeply and collectively committed to achieving in a mutually supportive way will succeed.

Other approaches—including dropping in charismatic *turnaround* leaders, dictating school personnel actions through mandates, and funding an initiative that was decided on by people outside of the community—will fall short of sustainable success (Leithwood, Harris, & Strauss, 2010). At best you gain compliance, but never commitment, and for only a short time. For this reason, a large-scale commitment is necessary for the success of *all* students.

7 TOOLS FOR CONSTRUCTING A LARGE-SCALE COMMUNITY COMMITMENT

The only winning, sustainable approach is the total engagement of the community in the new vision and in the process for reaching it. This begins by determining what the current practices are, the results achieved, and what the community wants to do about it. However, the difficult question remains: At what point and by what means do individuals commit to something?

THINK ABOUT IT

List the educational goals you have for your own biological children or another child you care deeply about. Now, think about the educational goals you have for the students in your school. How are the lists similar or different? Next, ask each community member to create two lists answering the same question. Are the items compatible? What are some courageous ideas that can be generated from the combined goals?

The community in the Vietnam vignette from Chapter 1 had the most compelling reason imaginable to commit to a new and promising process: their children. Although there are children at stake in our schools as well, professionals may see them as *those* children instead of *my* children. They may not see the connection between the education these children receive and their prospects for the future, or see how the future of their students is inextricably bound with everyone's future. Moreover, even if they understand that these are their children and that their future is determined each day in the school, they may not have the know-how or courage to do what it takes to succeed with each child.

Below are seven elements leadership can influence that are essential to creating large scale commitment in a community.

1. Ask questions to build connections to the vision and those creating it.

Again, the answer lies in the question. Depending on where the school is in its development, the questions will need to be very descriptive at first. In lower performing schools, it is more appropriate to find out what is happening *now*. What are the kids doing? What is working now? These and other "what" questions help do diagnosis, engage staff, yet keep the "lid" on (B. Portin & M. Knapp, personal communication, 2010).

Harriett Diaz, Principal of Renaissance Middle School, describes how she engaged her staff under tough circumstances: "It was just chaos, children were in the halls, there were no homerooms, kids wore coats all day, bells rang every 45 minutes, children were just constantly in the hall: every time a bell rang children were all over the hall. The teacher turnover was great; some didn't even stay a month. Some rooms had books in them, but I didn't see a lot of classroom libraries. Textbooks were rare, computers were available but were never turned on or used. It was just noisy and chaotic. I called the teachers in and simply asked: 'Why did you go into teaching in the first place?' Once we ignited the flame of why they got started, we tried to keep that flame burning."

Ms. Diaz didn't ask anything more at that staff meeting.

"We created a list of everything the school of our dreams would be. We then copied the list and put it in everyone's classrooms, bathrooms, everywhere. It was a constant reciting of what we were aiming for. And we had to stay to target, no matter what, I told them, 'I would pick up obstacles, anything that came in our way, let me carry that ball for you. We're just going to keep pushing ahead.'"

In other schools and districts such as Mansfield, Texas, and Fort Wayne, Indiana, the situation wasn't so dire, and the questions revolved more around the possibilities beyond all that had already been accomplished. What can we learn from the best? What would facilitate our getting to the next level?

Beginning the process by asking questions appropriate to the school setting repositions the leadership as learner, guide, and cocreator of a process that will allow the community to solve its own challenges. In short, the leader becomes a harmonizer of the community toward a common aim collectively identified as mission critical.

The assumption is that the leadership team is able to bring about an incisive answer to the question. This isn't always true initially. The answer to the question "What is the main problem we are facing?" may be "The parents!" If so, more questions and more data will need to be introduced. It may also be that another question needs to be posed: For example: "What specifically are the problems that are within *our* sphere to influence?"

Although people are defining their own and their collective course of action, they are vesting in the outcome. At the same time, using the proper tools, this process naturally builds the relationships across the school community, which is essential to sustainable success (Bryk et al., 2010).

2. Create the context for more "aha" moments.

In his recent book, *Giving Wings to Children's Dreams*, Paul Houston (2010), President, Center for Empowered Leadership and Executive Director, Emeritus, American Association of School Administrators (AASA), describes when he was a superintendent in Princeton and had a student who did virtually nothing in his school all day but hang out in the hallways and play the harmonica. One day a band director asked him to join the band, and the student replied that all he knew how to do was play the harmonica. The band director told him that was OK and he'd find music for the harmonica. The student is John Popper, now head of the Blues Travelers band. If Popper hadn't met this particular band director who took him in versus rejecting him, the student would likely have been another statistic. Ironically, Paul, once a failing student himself, was shocked to hear from a new teacher that he should consider becoming a writer! For both Houston and Popper, the "ahas" were life-changing and likely were "ahas" for their teachers as well. The personal connections were the secret to success.

Like Harriett Diaz, principal of Renaissance Middle School, Bronx, New York, signed up for a job in which each day that she showed up to school someone on the faculty would say, "You still here? I didn't think you were coming back!" But like Archbishop Tutu described previously, Harriett was personally connected to the children in that school in a way that would not lead to her being deterred. She was from that neighborhood and therefore able to relate and commit to the children in more than a generic sense—for her it was personal. Like Principal Wilson (Chapter 2), she too took that school from a D grade to an A status within 3 years.

The "aha" moments, whether or not they are literally in a moment, are those that tell the community member why they are committed to the other members of the group, notably the children. The leadership can help foster those moments by bringing members together in new and safe environments, celebrations, festivals, work settings, sporting events, and people's homes. It is often the case that "those students" become "my students" when a personal connection is formed. The leadership can make that more likely to occur. Likewise, the process described in this book is all about creating an environment in which personal and professional connections will thrive.

3. Assure short-term victories.

The CREATE process calls upon the same philosophy for getting started that Mel Riddle, former award-winning principal who turned around one of the worst schools in the state of Virginia, and now Title XX, used in his school: "I have two rules: I start small and only work with the willing."

Once the leadership has self-assessed and taken account of their capacity and major needs, goals will be collectively tailored for the group. Again, this is determined within the community, and external goals can be antithetical to this process as they are *one size fits all*. Clearly each community has different levels of capacity by contrast.

Christie Alfred, as the principal of Ben Barber Career and Technology Academy/ Frontier High School in the Mansfield Independent School District, started learning walks on a small scale and reframed them a "heart walk" during Valentine's Day. Those involved drew a teacher's name from a hat, watched another teacher for only 5 minutes, and left a note on the door using heart-shaped paper about only something positive they saw.

In general, very short-term goals should initially be set for groups with a history of failure or low-levels of self-efficacy. Principal Wilson merely dealt with making the procedure for walking in the halls and the bus dismissal orderly, for example.

For "cruising schools" (Stoll & Fink, 1996) that have a strong sense of efficacy, it is helpful to take another approach. Seeing a school with similar demographics but with much better student success outcomes, for example, may catalyze movement. The school may then commit to better outcomes for student performance, and building in short-term wins along the way would be wise.

Starting small with the willing, sharing and celebrating victories, and inviting others to join the game is a winning strategy for spreading what is working within the school community and for building positive relationships with others around that work.

4. Leverage early adopters.

Research by Albert Bandura on "vicarious learning" is fascinating and informative for anyone interested in bringing about change. Bandura initially developed the theory to get people to overcome great phobias. He engaged people who had a fear of snakes to watch others handle an anaconda. This made it possible for them to imagine it could be done and to overcome their fears about doing so. In small steps, he created a safe environment for observers to touch the snakes as well, and eventually handle them—all within 3 hours! Leveraging the early adopters to model a new teaching strategy, for example, is a key strategy in spreading positive deviance. Consider a "vicarious learning" strategy your community could implement to scale up student success?

5. See-do-believe yourself into codifying new behaviors.

The new behavior—not outcome of a behavior—is what must be clearly defined for change to occur. For example a school team may watch a teacher who is successful with students whom others send to the principal's office. Maybe they discover that her high-leverage behaviors have to do with how she quietly and efficiently addresses them when they act out. Were this the case, that behavior would become the focus for others to practice and enhance in their own classrooms. This is different from staff being told to "improve relations with students" or "don't send students out of the room so easily!"

Modeling as mentioned above is a critical next step and can come in the form of visiting another school or classroom. Next, the new behavior has to be tried by the practitioner. It is at this point that the process of change really begins. With proper coaching, feedback, and review of the successes derived from that new behavior, new beliefs start to develop: "Oh, those kids really CAN learn!" Without this process, it is easier for old beliefs to remain intact, as they lead to the same outcomes due to use of the same self-reinforcing behaviors. So the intervention is in defining and then changing the high-leverage behaviors that will lead to new results, followed by new beliefs. What are the specific high-yield behaviors your school community can leverage?

6. Create the context for success.

"When an army has the force of momentum, even the timid become brave; when it loses momentum, even the brave become timid" (Tzu, 2005, p. 97).

Collectively, it will make sense for educators to come together with other leaders vested in the future of our children and form local and national understandings around the need for those who literally shape the future to be treated as a respected group of professionals. This would greatly enhance the ability of those professionals to define and solve their own challenges.

At the district level, many of the same challenges exist that we see at the national level. It is hard to even fund a sustainable initiative when so much money is focused on short-term gain. Maurice Elias, Professor of Psychology at Rutgers University, explains that "money-starved states have their eye on federal dollars that will soon dry up. In the meantime, they basically do whatever the feds require and this combination makes commitment to systemic change difficult." He calls it "short-term entrepreneurialism (personal communication, 2011)."

Nonetheless, it is imperative that within whatever sphere one is operating, the context for success is created. The district leaders with whom we have worked, for example, have been *imaginative* in pooling and recategorizing funds so that it makes sense to create a robust, committed group of leaders with the capacity to not only launch but to sustain their efforts.

Relations with the larger community, families, and the school board are all a part of assessing and aligning the terrain for success. As Wendy Robinson, Superintendent of Fort Wayne Community Schools, said relative to their success: "We're going to do the right thing because it's the right thing to do. But I couldn't have done all this without the tremendous support I have from the board." How can your community create the context for success in your school, your district, your state, and your nation?

7. When necessary, circumvent the system.

Courageous leaders find a way to do what is right versus finding creative ways to explain why doing the wrong thing is still not working. In many instances, the principals interviewed, for example, demonstrated their commitment to the success of their students by shielding them and their teaching staff from deleterious practices. Using what Seymour Fliegel calls "creative non-compliance" Anne Bryant, Executive Director of the National School Boards Association, sees excellent practices in virtually every district but also sees rules that impede the scaling of them! "A lot of rules that are state, locally or federally driven make no sense, and we just refuse to break them!" (Personal communication, 2010.)

One principal of a now high-performing school, for example, simply hid the new curriculum she was mandated to use because she knew it wouldn't work for her students. Another tried to follow the research on the need for late starting times for his high school students but was stymied repeatedly by district policies. The school instead changed the schedule to make all the hard core courses in the afternoon, and "performance skyrocketed."

It is unfortunate that there are so many obstacles put in the path of educators to effectively do their job. Yet amazingly, effective school communities find their way around them!

CREATE AND COURAGEOUS LEADERSHIP

Qualities of the Courageous Leader

Endeavoring systemic change over time is not for the faint hearted—it's for the successful heroes and ardent advocates of our children. As a courageous leader, here are some of the qualities that are helpful to cultivate toward this success.

- **Learn how to win the battle before beginning it.** There is an old Chinese story about three brothers who practice medicine. One is known throughout the country because he is able to reverse severe situations among the critically ill. The second brother is known throughout the province because he is able to restore very sick patients to good health. The third is only known by close friends and family because he helps them maintain high-functioning diets and energy flow that prevent most illness, and he spots and intervenes quickly when things go awry. Honing in on a clear, high-leverage strategy is key to deriving maximum benefits for students. It takes time, focus, proper analysis, and managing distractions. "Education systems believe they should respond to the ever changing, rapidly multiplying, broadly diverse needs and demands of many constituent groups" (Wagner et al., 2005). Consider this alternative:

We often need to reframe or redefine the problem to solve it. This generally takes a deeper analysis on the part of the learning community, and highly skilled guidance from the leader or leadership team.

"We have the community define the big issue they are facing and then solve one smaller (high-leverage) aspect of it. In Clairton, Pennsylvania, outside of Pittsburgh, the highway bypasses the town. There are economic problems and a high incidence of violence among teens. We are still in the inquiry phase now, but when we first asked school personnel about the nature of the problems youth are facing, they identify it as violence. If you ask the students, many of them give another answer: being suspended for tardiness. Those suspensions lead to a lot of angry young people being on the street with nothing to do" (M. Sternin, personal communication, 2011).

From her experience with Jerry Sternin in Vietnam, Monique is used to researching complex issues and reconceptualizing the *problem* in new, actionable terms. In this case, it may be that the *youth violence* issue will be greatly reduced by changes in suspension policy. The literature is filled with such high-leverage, often simple solutions to seemingly complex and intractable problems (Patterson et al., 2008). The challenge then becomes how to get people to *implement* what is known to be effective, and the CREATE process as a *whole* is designed to address this.

The previous example would be akin to the second Chinese brother's actions, as he intervenes quickly and effectively after the problem has arisen. Another aspect of CREATE is embedding the process, the new thinking, and the capacity for action in the learning community such that such interventions are often unnecessary. Hypothetically extending the case of youth violence discussed previously, early surveying of young people and addressing alternatives to suspension in the overall school planning and school culture would be akin to how the third Chinese brother prevents illness.

- **Just do it.** Perhaps the best way to end the new initiative is to name it, have a pronouncement ceremony, announce it to the press, and share it with the community. As Mel Riddle states: "Most people go in and announce what they are going to do . . . without getting data or teachers' opinions, and they get a lot of resistance as a result. We did the assessments, presented data, and asked for volunteers to work on it. We built our successes with that experimental group and in so doing gained the confidence of others necessary to spread it throughout the school." This is exactly the process coming chapters will expand upon relative to the district-level work as well.

   Common responses to pronouncements of new initiatives are sabotage and renaming old approaches with the latest slogan. By the time the next leader comes on board, the staff can confidently announce: "Yep, we did learning communities last year already!"

- **Let the sun shine.** If the leader can see her shadow, she is blocking the sun. Sometimes the tallest tree in the forest can stunt the growth of the trees around it. For this reason it is hard to sustain success built around a single leader's presence. Principal E. Kent Mertz of Waynedale Elementary School, in Fort Wayne, said: "When you are hiring, it's increasingly more important to find someone who can work well with that team. It used to be that we would just hire the best teachers. I don't look for superstars anymore; I look for people who can augment, not usurp, the team." Being a part of the community team will be more important to the successful outcome than will be having a powerful presence whether that person is a teacher or administrator at the building or district level.

- **Take powerful action through stillness.** In the book *Flow* (Csikszentmihalyi, 1990), athletes hit peak performance at certain times when they are internally calm and still, and everything coming at them seems to slow down. We have all seen the opposite—someone who is nervous or hysterical and can't seem to decide which way to move. That person may leave the house quickly in the morning, yet have to return three times to get forgotten items. Speed is only powerful when it's focused. And focus comes out of stillness.

- **Maintain control by letting go.** Lightning bugs are beautiful for children to see and they therefore often wind up in glass containers. While "in the wild," fireflies only live 3 days (the second day is generally when they mate), in captivity they die much sooner. They also don't mate in captivity, so the beauty of the light the children admire and want to capture is ironically extinguished prematurely. Similarly, the CREATE process is extinguished if not allowed to follow its natural course. Although the leader helps define that course, it is done using an empowering process that is ultimately owned and continuously improved by the community. By letting this process and the people in it thrive, everyone reaps the rewards of having more than one or a few lightbulbs turning on in the room. Getting to the mutually desired outcome is most likely when the leadership allows the process to work.

- **Practice full engagement and detachment.** In the *Power of Full Engagement* (Loehr & Schwartz, 2003), there is an irony discovered that accounts for why some athletes outperform others of similar skill. It has to do with how they manage their energy. The most successful ones take frequent breaks—even during a match—so that they can go the distance. So full engagement requires an emotional detachment at times in order to better assess the situation, intervene in tough situations without exacerbating them, or give difficult feedback to colleagues and employees about performance in a neutral, data-based manner. Without detachment, burnout is the likely alternative.

- **Maintain constancy and clarity of purpose.** This third axiom of Courageous Leadership (Blankstein, 2004/2010) is critical to success and was originally derived from our work with W. Edwards Deming, the quality guru who changed the world. Yet it is seldom practiced in our leader and *program du jour* society. In *So Much Reform, So Little Change,* Charles Payne explains.
- "The revolving door of leadership in most schools and districts creates a problem because one does not develop relationships over time" (Tony Wagner with AB, No. 22). Rapid succession of leadership is common and takes a devastating toll on initiatives to affect student learning (Louis, Leithwood, Wahlstrom, & Anderson, 2010).

THE BIG QUESTION

What Core Commitment Is Your Community Prepared to Make?

This chapter focused on the first and most critical element to any major school community: leadership. The type of leadership needed to bring about large-scale, sustainable improvements has also been proposed in this chapter. In addition, some of the activities undertaken by the leadership team have also been defined. The next chapter will focus more clearly on defining the external challenges to large-scale change and how courageous, committed leaders galvanize the necessary resources to succeed.

Resources
Are in the Room

"Even if well intentioned, attempting to do everything at once drains resources and energy from educators and gets little results."

—Doug Reeves (2007)

The resources required to do the kind of work described in this book are much more valuable than money and perhaps harder to come by in a chaotic educational environment. In fact, the monetary cost of sharing excellence across a district is far less than hiring a series of keynote speakers and far more productive. The most effective professional development is sustained, in-depth, and embedded (Darling-Hammond, Wei, Andree, Richardson, & Orphanos, 2009).

As Gail Cooper, Principal of Pottstown Middle School in Pennsylvania, explained: "Previously the school brought in outside consultants for their professional development sessions. Although they were very good, many teachers didn't relate. I'd overhear them saying: 'That wouldn't work in our school.'" Cooper says it was "a study in frustration." "The new approach to tapping and sharing (positive deviance) through networks is much more satisfying," says Cooper. "They like learning from their peers and sharing their expertise. They inspire each other." See Figure 4.1 and Figure 4.2 for the gains in math and reading at Pottstown Middle School in Pottstown, Pennsylvania.

Figure 4.1 Pottstown Middle School Math Proficiency Passing Rates 2008–2010

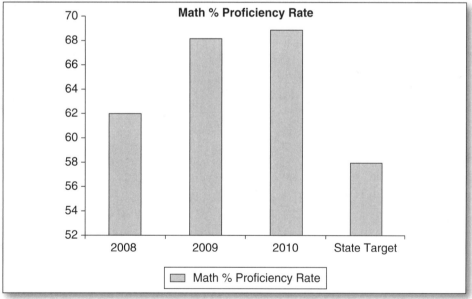

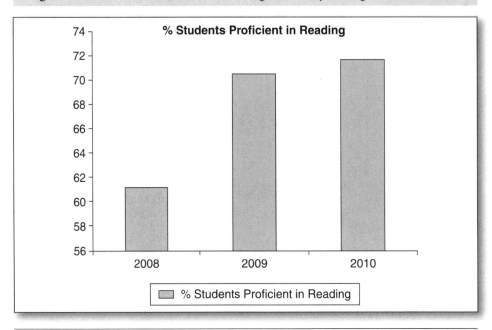

Figure 4.2 Pottstown Middle School Reading Proficiency Passing Rates 2008–2010

Reprinted with permission.

In June 2008 schoolwide math scores at Pottstown middle school were 62% proficient or above. The next year they were able to raise that number to 68.2% and then to 68.9% in 2010. State target scores for proficient or above is 56% in math. Overall the district made adequate yearly progress (AYP) for the past 2 years for the first time in its 15-year history. African-American students outperformed their white counterparts in math. Similar results are shown in reading, starting out at 61.3% in 2008, rising to 70.6% the next year and then to 71.8% in 2010.

THE MOST VALUABLE RESOURCE: FOCUSED COMMITMENT OVER TIME

Although financial costs are involved with providing a well-honed process for leveraging what is working throughout the school community and to engage everyone in *implementing* those practices, they are relatively minimal. When the community itself becomes the expert, costs for external gurus goes down as does travel and materials costs. The external expertise needed is in understanding the process and facilitating it.

The *most* important resource to be allocated is actually a *commitment and focus over a sustained period of time.* This kind of focus is required by the *sponsors* of the effort—those with the economic, political, and logistical power to support change. With that in place, the rest will follow. However, many obstacles exist to bringing these resources to fruition. Consider just a few:

- **Educational experts abound.** What has been shared in virtually every district in which we have begun this process is that leaders in these schools and districts have been called upon so frequently by so many vendors. With such delightful, marvelous *solutions* it becomes difficult to say no all the time and confusing as to when to say yes! Many of these companies are for-profit, and a surprising number don't even have a track record or a valid third-party evaluation of the efficacy of their work. They rely instead on who knows whom, who knows you. If a Martian landed in the United States from outer space, it would have only to review how many recent entrants there are to the school *turn-around* market to know that a new major grant was given for . . . yes, turning around schools!

  The question is, how many *gurus* does it take to help school leaders run a powerful internal exchange around what's working? And unfortunately for those gurus, the answer is close to none. So there is little incentive for many corporate interests to support such an idea.

- **We suffer an acute case of *program-itus.*** What if programs really didn't easily solve problems? What would we as professionals have left to rely on?

  There is a joke about a principal who prayed for help and opened his eyes to see the ghost of John Dewey.

  "What are you doing here?" the principal asked.

  Dewey replied: "You asked for help and they sent me. Let's get on with it, shall we?!" The principal explained his challenges.

  Dewey knowingly responded: "We can address this in the ordinary way, or in the miraculous way."

  The principal asked for details about the "ordinary way."

  Dewey replied: "Well, we send down a hundred angels; all of time stands still for a moment; darkness fills the sky and then is lifted as the angels ascend to the heavens and your problems are gone."

  Principal: "Wow! That's the 'ordinary' way?! What's the 'miraculous' way to solve my problems?"

  Dewey: "YOU do it!"

  We have become a community of shoppers, seeking off-the-shelf, push-button, homogenized, and money-back-guaranteed solutions to all of our problems. As with any addiction, we are invariably disappointed when the high wears off because the solutions don't quite endure. Unfortunately, the original problems still loom, and there's even less in our budget to address them.

Let the rehabilitation begin! There are no *solutions,* and programs only work in limited contexts. "The solution is not a program: It is a small set of common principles and practices relentlessly pursued" (Fullan, 2010, p. 59). *Solutions* and *programs* do not fit every context, and are not *owned* by those using them. A good process, by contrast, is designed to engage the users in cocreating answers to their own challenges. So, programs and people (like charismatic leaders) who eventually depart and leave in place a reliant, often weak team are not sustainable. Good processes and principles can work in different contexts and engage the entire learning community.

Yet our collective addiction to easy, simple solutions is also fed by funding streams that will soon dry up (M. Elias, personal communication, 2010). The looming crisis in Vietnam that led to that country inviting Save the Children to address child malnutrition was that the subsidies were about to end. More than a decade of external funding and food shipments to prop that country up was coming to a close, leaving an even more impoverished reliant and underempowered population to its own devices. Leveraging the "wisdom in the room" via a community-driven approach to identifying the answer it already possessed and then scaling it provided an antidote to that problem, as it built capacity for solving other challenges.

Even if the recent infusion of educational funds continued forever, the traditional approach to their use would be unproductive because they do not build the capacity of the learning community to solve its own problems and bring that to scale. In short "The stimulus money, *in the absence of an appropriate whole system reform conception,* will fail" (Fullan, 2010, p. 29).

- **False mapping will lead to dead ends, and both distract us from a meaningful focus.** "It's better to have a good question than an answer" explained W. Edwards Deming (1989) because how that question is framed will greatly influence our understanding of the problem and the trajectory of attending actions. If we ask, "What will it take for these kids to do better on their tests?" for example, we are likely to come up with an array of test-taking strategies. If we ask instead, "What will it take to fully engage our students in learning?" we will likely develop a very exciting school culture and authentic, relevant curriculum that leads students, as a by-product, to doing well on their tests.
- **Leaders' tenure is generally short.** Who can focus on an initiative if hiring and retraining are consistently at the top of the agenda? Constancy of purpose is tied to constancy of leadership and both are critical to success.
- **The ground beneath educators shifts regularly.** Given the political undulations that swing educators from focusing on making sure none of their students are illegal one day, to dealing with a new merit pay idea the next, it is easy to see why focus is hard to come by. Yet effective learning communities carve out space to

focus on a few key priorities, while *managing* the distractions. The CREATE process is inherently helpful in this as depth and breadth of commitment to solving the community's problem is built in from the beginning.

All of the previously stated challenges (and many more) make it equally understandable that school communities both yearn for, and look suspiciously at the latest focus of the leadership. Yet this is exactly why the CREATE process is needed all the more.

Where we have seen success, sustained commitment and focus have usually developed iteratively over some period of time. That is, the district leader or curriculum supervisor or staff developer became aware of a way of moving the district forward. They then expose others to that information and get feedback. At a certain point, enough support exists within the community that a decision is made to go forward. This same scenario can start with a principal or anyone else in the community, as long as that person knows how to engage others and move it up to the top *sponsors*.

THE SECOND MAJOR RESOURCE: PATIENCE AND URGENCY

The second resource that is required combines patience and a sense of urgency. The urgency comes in immediately doing everything possible to move the community forward within the process. The patience comes with honoring that process. For example, many at this phase realized the importance of preparing the entire community before yet another launch of a new initiative. This often came in the form of a book study, although other means of getting people to understand the process to come may have included visiting other sites, bringing someone in, and other forms of professional development. The Pottstown district preceded its book study with an ice cream social and invited all staff to learn more about the system. The motto adhered to was "slow is smooth and smooth is fast."

Once the ground was laid and the school community had time to discuss the new direction, what burning needs it would address, and how it would likely unfold, the decision was made collectively to commit time, energy, and focus. Realizing that so many staff had doubts about the follow-through of yet another initiative, these sponsors proceeded with urgency, yet patience and wisdom to assure the sustainability of the effort.

THE THIRD MAJOR RESOURCE: STEERING COMMITTEE

The steering committee is formed to align internal activities and to guide and interface with external experts in the process. It usually consists of the district *sponsors* and often includes someone charged with data collection and reporting, school or community-based leaders, and/or leaders of other infrastructures already in place in the district. (e.g., in Wichita, every school had a coach, and those coaches became integral to implementation of this process and were therefore represented on the committee to ensure coordination of efforts). Regular planning and evaluation of the process by the committee is preceded by helping to create and guide school-based leadership teams. These teams come together to do the work described in the rest of the CREATE process.

Sarah Jandrucko, Area Superintendent, Mansfield Independent School District (ISD), from the steering committee of Mansfield ISD, shares the experience of the initial steps of getting the principals and then the school-based teams together:

> Step one is very simplistic. We gathered everyone together in one location and sat them at a round table so they were all physically facing one another. Initially, in many cases it's forced; you are forcing people to come together and be in close proximity with one another. For high schools it's huge! We were serving pizza at the high school, and we saw two women chatting instead of getting their pizza. We asked them, and they said, "We never get to see each other; we're on different sides of the building." When you have such large schools, as most high schools are, even in middle schools, people don't have an opportunity to come together. This project made us come together as a team, and we came together either across grade levels or across disciplines, and that's very unusual. Most of the time, the principal gathers you in a faculty meeting where everyone is in the room, but she's only delivering information.

The interesting thing about this process is that sometimes *it* becomes the catalyst to people actually meeting one another. As in the previous story, it is often the case that people in the same building, much less within an entire district, simply don't meet. If trust across the learning community is essential to high performance in a school—and it is—then how would it be present if people didn't even know one another? This phase of the process alone begins to create the likelihood of success, as it engenders relationships that didn't previously exist.

The school-based leadership team is formed directly following this phase. Although most schools already have such teams in place, they frequently are not ideal for advancing sustainable success. One common reason is that the teams are not representative of the school, but rather of the leader who created them. Although this is great for *launching* an effort, those who are not well represented will sooner than later bring that launch back down to the ground with a thud. Choosing the right team, even with reasonable *naysayers*—not career saboteurs—is essential for success over time.

Sarah Jandrucko adds: "If you have everybody working on the problem in collaboration with one another, then I think performance in time will improve. We're a 'recognized' district in the state of Texas this year. And I think that's directly related to the fact that we're sharing more than we've ever shared before, we're collaborating more than we've ever collaborated before, and more people are involved in the discussion than ever before."

HOW TO GET TIME TO COLLABORATE

Darling-Hammond and colleagues (2009) found that American teachers spend more time teaching students and have less time to plan and learn together in developing high-quality curriculum and instruction than teachers in other nations. Furthermore, U.S. teachers spend about 80% of their total working time engaged in classroom instruction, as compared to about 60% of their counterparts in other nations (Darling-Hammond et al., 2009).

 In the *Tools to Help Answer the Questions in the Room* in the back of this book, there is a checklist of "Strategies for Making Time" in Tool B.

Finding time to collaborate is a common obstacle and completely legitimate. At the same time, it is crucial in building trust, commitment, and common mission, values, and goals. Not having the time can be a smokescreen for staff who may not want to take part in the process. Some questions that may be asked to *resisters* to uncover their underlying reasons include the following:

- Is time the only issue?
- If I were to assure you that you will have sufficient time, would you become actively involved in the process?

The key to working with resisters is that their time must be seen as well spent (Blankstein, 2004/2010). Tool B offers a starting list for finding and making time.

GETTING DOWN TO THE DETAILS

Once the sponsorship's focus and commitment are solid, the groundwork for community engagement has been laid, and the steering committee and effective school leadership teams are in place, the traditional definition of "resources" can be addressed. This list of resources will vary from one location to another; however, there is often a fair amount of consistency. The important insight here is that these *traditional* resources can be named and more easily *obtained* once the sponsors of the effort and entire learning community have focused on and committed to addressing a challenge of great importance to them.

Figure 4.3 is a combined list from two different districts engaged in this work.*

Figure 4.3 Combined List of Resources

Commitment to all children succeeding through building leadership teams, owning the corporation vision, and creating an action plan to reach success.

Time for collaboration must be allotted with support for how collaboration can share leadership and attain goals.

(Continued)

Figure 4.3 (Continued)

People resources—curriculum, student services, school improvement coordination, PD, and coaches who are willing to come to the building and work with the staff.

Data and/or assessment systems must be embedded into the daily practice of instruction, planning, and ongoing PD for areas of need.

Expectations must be made clear. Not all buildings will look alike, but there are expectations for every building.

Technology that works and is actually being used such as online assessment, portable labs, and so on.

Patience and tolerance are required as people learn through the change process with support of district/school coaches working with area administration.

Training for linking state standards to ongoing planned instruction, data, collaboration, and professional development in the student success model.

*Adapted from Jason Short, Principal, Asa E. Low Jr., Intermediate School, Mansfield Independent School District, Mansfield, TX; Carolyn Powers, Director of Elementary Administration, Fort Wayne Community Schools, Fort Wayne, IN.

THE BIG QUESTION

What would it take for your school community to commit the three major resources above (focused commitment over time; patience and urgency; steering committee) to a sustained improvement effort? Who in the school community would be the sponsors of this process?

The important issue comes back to leadership, in this chapter reframed as *sponsorship*. The same issues addressed in the prior chapter that lead to success are echoed in this chapter as well: commitment, focus, engagement of the larger community, and developing a common understanding of the problem and vision for addressing it. When these things are in place, anything can be accomplished. The boxed list above becomes merely details to be addressed, rather than obstacles for halting the movement forward. The next chapter spotlights the process of defining excellence so that it may become the norm in the entire school community.

Taking Stock of the Excellence in the Room

> *"The formulation of the problem is often more essential than its solution."*
> —Albert Einstein

*T*he Answer Is in the Room is the idea that within every community there lies not only a problem, but also a solution to that problem. This chapter describes how a *group* of

Figure 5.1 Leadership Teams

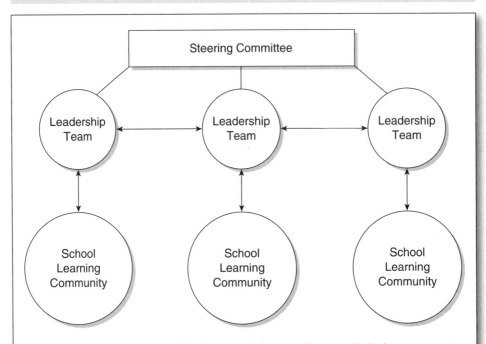

Leadership teams convened by the steering committee regularly learn processes for identifying and scaling positive deviance. In turn, they use them at their school sites and bring back with them artifacts of what they learned in their school learning community. This is then shared across the learning teams to scale those practices across the district.

educators actually become a team, and how that team helps to build their respective learning community. The development of high-performing teams and their common language for, and ability to identify, excellent practice is the next step prior to scaling that practice. In addition, for the *community* to define excellence, it must first be formed intentionally. Gathering a group of smart professionals or certain top-level individuals to point out what is working and tell others to replicate it is not sufficient; the excellence must be identified by and within the community itself.

Much of this chapter is dedicated to the development of the learning or leadership teams and their use within the larger districtwide networking construct (see Figure 5.1, indicating how these teams interact with both the steering committee and their respective school communities). Before these teams can seek outliers of excellence in their schools they must define excellence and agree among themselves on that definition. By having this common language, they can then also communicate across the entire district about what positive deviance they have found, such that they can plan to bring it to scale both in their schools and across the district or region. This development of common language and definitions begins in the Courageous Leadership Academy through the use of certain tools provided below. Before any of this can happen, however, the teams must be formed. Before addressing the formulation of teams, it is helpful to reestablish what they are likely to find, and how they must engage their larger learning communities to find it.

IS THERE EXCELLENCE OR POSITIVE DEVIANCE TO BE FOUND?

In speaking with top educational researchers, policymakers, and practitioners about this concept, virtually every single person agreed that pockets of excellence can be found in any school community. (Although two experts indicated that it depended on the size and definition of the community.) Almost all the interviewees shared concerns about the challenges in scaling student success or spreading those "random acts of excellence" (T. Wagner, personal communication, 2010) across the system. Most of those concerns the experts voiced were around the inability of a school community to transfer the knowledge they have because of cultural barriers, lack of trust, isolation, and other interpersonal concerns.

Phil Schlecty and Tony Wagner indicated that most of what we are striving for in America is not adequate to address what Wagner refers to as the "Global Achievement Gap." Instead, we should teach essential "survival skills," such as critical thinking and problem-solving (Wagner, 2008).

DEFINING EXCELLENCE IS DONE TWICE BY THE LEAD TEAMS

Finding and scaling what's working in the community requires a different type of leadership than that which has been the norm in our society. In Chapter 3, new leadership qualities that relate to leading an *inside-out process* were discussed. In more traditional reform models, the leader has the answer and shares that with the *subordinates,* who then implement the ideas. In more recent reform approaches, the leader has the answer and then tries to get everyone else to guess it or state it, and thereby gets buy-in. This leads to even greater distrust than had the leader shared the answer in the first place! There is a third way: one in which *the question is the answer and the process is actually the strategy.*

This approach to leadership can be difficult to put into practice as our culture demands a strong forceful leader with all the answers. As discussed in Chapter 2, it takes *real* strength and courage to instead do what works, beginning with asking smart questions, convening groups to answer questions, and using the CREATE process to facilitate community commitment to acting on those answers.

Getting the answer to *what* we should do—the technical stuff—is easy. Remember that Jerry Sternin and his team in Vietnam found out within a couple of months what some outlier families did to nourish their children while the rest of the young children were starving. And as Pascale and colleagues wrote, coming up with this part of the solution is only

20% of the job (Pascale, Sternin, & Sternin, 2010). Likewise, in education, we could convene a small leadership team and in a couple of hours have consensus around what needs to be done: For example, "We need a system for collecting and giving us real-time data," "We need to strengthen students' literacy skills," or "We need to close the gap between white and non-white students." If we only answer the what needs to be done question, we will likely put in place a lot of new structures (i.e., days for professional learning community (PLC) teams to meet, a timeline for deciding the school improvement plan, a new literacy curriculum) and a new infrastructure (e.g., new computers, new bus schedule, additional teaching assistants). Yet, we would still have the same culture, relationships, trust issues, and conversations. In addition, by answering the *what* question in a small group, the individuals who come up with the answer now own the solution and its implementation while everyone else in the community gets to watch!

The hardest part of the equation is answering the "how?" question in a manner that engages the community. This involves facilitating the school community in answering their own questions around *how*? In other words, that process itself *is* the answer. Once the answer to the problems of malnourishment had been discovered by Jerry Sternin (i.e., feeding infants small shrimp, using better hygiene techniques), the research team had to ask the rest of the community how to share this in a manner that would be acceptable and productive for *them* to change their behavior. That question was part of the answer as it engaged the people with the problem in finding the solution (Pascale et al., 2010).

This book's approach is far different than creating yet another strategic plan and getting *buy-in* to implement it. The difference is that all members of the community are part of the solution. Therefore, the leadership teams learn about and practice tools for defining and then finding good practice during their CLA meetings, and then do this once again within their schools.

DEVELOPING A COMMUNITY TO QUESTION THE ANSWER

Language, Purpose, and Norms

Using a Common Language

To get started, it is helpful for the steering committee and the leadership or learning teams to have a common language and framework for action. In the case examples in this book, the common system and framework for action has been the six principles of Failure Is Not an Option® (see Figure 2.1), but other frameworks may also be used.

Figure 5.2 indicates how these six principles work together as a system. An important concept to remember is that the learning or leadership teams should be oriented to the framework they are using to help bring cohesion to the work *already* underway in schools and to provide a common language for discussing the work.

In Figure 5.2, each of the six principles is interdependent and connected. When one moves, it acts as a lever to turn the others as well. So, for example, when the common Mission, Vision, Values, and Goals are properly created, leadership capacity is also built. Since the principles allow for a comprehensive view of what is already underway in the learning community and common language for discussing it, the community can more effectively decide future priorities, define excellence, and scale it when it is found. Given prior resources allocated (Chapter 4), effective leadership (Chapter 3), and the steering committee in place, those teams now convene and begin to get in synch as to why they are there.

Figure 5.2 *Failure Is Not an Option®*: System COGS

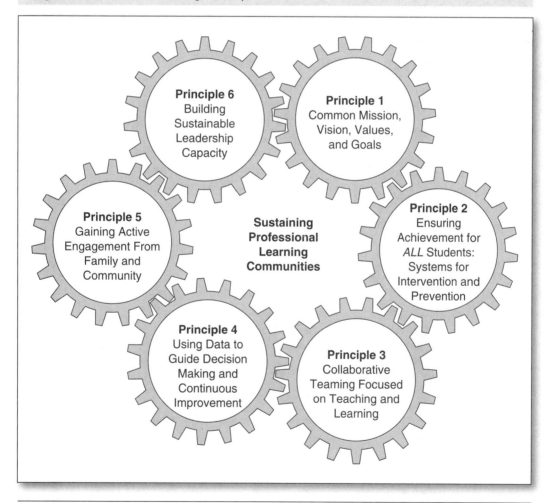

Developing a Common Purpose

Traditional reform approaches in professional development call for a brief statement by the leader as to why everyone is there. The leader would generally depart so that the workshop can proceed while she gets some *important* work done! In keeping with this CREATE methodology, however, this new approach to leadership comes from those in the room and the top-level leaders generally stay and *participate* (not watch). Their participation not only sends a powerful message to all involved of the importance of the work, it also enhances that work in two ways. (1) If the lead learners are not in the room, the *answer* that is derived as to how best move forward is potentially less powerful than it otherwise would be. (2) Having everyone in the room makes it more likely that the "final two percent"—the element of total commitment, passion, trust, and synergy of the *entire* learning community that comes only when people are working side-by-side—will be a part of the equation. That final two percent is what distinguishes great from good performances (D. Sparks, personal communication, 2010).

 In the *Tools to Help Answer the Questions in the Room,* you will find the "Agreement of Purpose Worksheet" as Tool C.

Agreeing on Purpose

The Agreement of Purpose is a structure and process to define and facilitate shared purpose as well as prioritize goals to guide the work of the community. Benefits of the agreement of purpose:

- Ensures that everyone agrees on the purpose and process for the work.
- Gives a context for decision making.
- Provides a yardstick to measure progress.
- Focuses collaboration and planning.

Figure 5.3   Steps to Developing Your Agreement of Purpose

Step 1:

- Form pairs or triads within your school leadership team (SLT).
- In your pair or triad, share your response to the first Agreement of Purpose Worksheet question: "From my point of view, the primary purpose of our SLT working as a professional learning community is. . . ."
- Identify the common ground among your statements and any powerful words you think need to be used.
- Together develop a statement that reflects the shared purpose of your SLT.

Step 2:

- Join the pairs and triads of your SLT together and share the statement of purpose each pair/triad created.
- Identify the common ground among the statements and power words you think need to be used.
- Create a new statement of purpose that reflects the combined thinking of the SLT and is supported by all members.
- Write your SLT's statement of purpose on chart paper and post on the wall.

Step 3:

- Each SLT member shares what they have written for Question 2 on their Agreement of Purpose Worksheet: "I offer the following expertise and commitment to working as an SLT and moving toward our shared purpose. . . ."

Process to Identify Goals

Step 4: Identifying Goals

- Share your responses to the third question related to goals/priorities.
- Each person selects his top three to four goals and writes each one on a separate sticky note.
- As you write out your top three to four goals place each one on the table.
- As each person adds to the list, begin to group similar goals together to create affinity groupings.
- Once all goals have been placed into affinity groups, write a goal statement for each affinity group and record it on a chart paper.

Step 5: Prioritizing Goals

- Each person will be given 3 colored sticky dots.
- Review the goals listed and identify the goal(s) that are a priority for you by placing your colored sticky dots on those goal(s).
- You may place all 3 dots on one goal, or disperse them among 2 or 3 goals.
- Identify the top priority goals that are reflected by the colored dots.
- As a follow up activity, you may wish to combine some of the goals that have been grouped together and write a revised goal statement incorporating all of them together.

Step 6:

- Record your Agreement of Purpose Statement and your Priority Goals.

There are two things to note here relative to *purpose.* If we only graduate proficiency-driven test takers, we will have failed our children. Their joy in learning must be exponentially enhanced by their school experience, not doused by their ability to demonstrate recall on a test. Not only will this mind-deadening approach extinguish the flames of passion for learning and striving for excellence, but at its worst, it leads to disconnect, which has multiple ramifications for students' behavior in class and success in life. Ironically, being overly focused on the test is not even a good way to assure good test scores (Phillips, 2009).

Second, the team must be the ones to define its purpose. Although this invariably goes on within the context of whatever governmental mandates may exist, those mandates alone will usually not be sufficient to catalyze energetic forward motion. At best, external mandates are met with minimal compliance (Block, 2008; Deming, 1982; Pink, 2009; Senge, 2006). This is contrary to the kind of results we have observed when using this process correctly and allowing the community to create a more intrinsically motivating purpose. In these cases, external measures—like adequate yearly progress or EQAO—become a floor, not a ceiling for the community.

Defining the Team Meeting Norms

Groups of educators often come together without knowing exactly why or how to achieve the purpose when it is known. This can lead to anything from a gripe session to turning to pleasant matters such as arranging for the field trip. As E. Kent Martz, Principal of Waynedale Elementary School in Fort Wayne, Indiana, describes:

> Prior to training, a team of teachers used to sit down, go around the table and ask, "Do you have anything you would like to share?" Teachers shared anything on their minds around the topic at hand and would offer support and help to one another. They might have brought up, for example, the rehearsal for a Christmas program. They would then determine who will do what and when it needs to be done in order to have a good presentation. They dealt more on the management of a program or school function.

By contrast, the aforementioned team and others using CREATE begin to get clear on their collective focus as well as state-of the-art tools for discussing issues around instruction, for example, so that they can scale what they have collectively determined is excellent practice. Creating basic purpose and norms for meeting conversations are two pillars for teams to productively dialogue. This, along with having a common framework for discussing work, then allows for collectively determining problem areas and defining excellence around student achievement. The team now has a clear focus on student data and changing instruction for improving student achievement.

Creating Norms

One tool that has been used to develop this common understanding of team is shown in Figure 5.4. This tool is one of many that could be used to help develop a

Figure 5.4   Purpose of Norms

The Purpose of Norms help groups build trust by doing the following:

- Creating a climate that makes it safe to challenge
- Being creative
- Taking risks
- Allowing for satisfying, important work to occur

Norms support the opportunity to do the following:

- Engage in deep, insightful conversations
- Listen
- Help ensure time together is well spent

common language around how those engaged will communicate with one another; what is the reason for their
work together; what are their common mission, vision,
values, and goals. It offers a process to optimize collaborative teaming.

 In the *Tools to Help Answer the Questions in the Room,* you will find "Creating Group Norms" in Tool D and an "An Example Participant Handout for Creating Group Norms" in Tool E.

IMPROVING INSTRUCTIONAL PRACTICE

Change the Methods and You Will Change the Outcomes

With common language, purpose, and norms cocreated by the leadership or learning
group, the pillars for becoming a real team are in place. The process for creating each of
these using the tools above, moreover, helps to build trust among the now forming teams.
Now these teams are ready to tackle tasks that are directly related to finding and scaling
excellence throughout the school community. This begins with defining excellence so that
they may look for PD in their respective schools while again building more relational
trust.

It is important to note two things in this process:

1. The defining of good practice described below is the first step in allowing us
   to look for new behaviors in the school and classrooms—high-leverage or
   vital behaviors we will eventually want to bring to scale. This allows us also
   to depersonalize practice and get away from ego-centered obstacles to
   improvement.

2. The tools and discussions referenced in this chapter have thus far been used only
   among the leadership teams meeting across the CLA. How to get them to become
   widespread, and means of defining, identifying, and then scaling PD is taken up
   in the next chapters.

As discussed in Chapter 2, quality guru W. Edwards Deming indicated there are five
inputs to any system and that one could predict or alter the system's *outcomes* by changing
the inputs (Deming, 1982). They are as follows: people, environment, method, machines,
and materials used.

It is interesting to note that he also said that "people" were not the first place to turn
when trying to improve inputs to the system and that getting "better" people into a
system that wasn't working, would have only a minor impact on the outcomes of that
system (Deming, 1982). The input we are focusing on in this chapter, and to a great
extent throughout this book, is *method.* So the theory of action is this: There are very
few, if any, bad people in education. Generally, there are good people using bad

methods. If we change the methodology, we change the outcomes. To change the methodology, we need to do more than show people a better method and tell them to "do it." We need to also create the proper climate for mutual trust, support, and accountability. This process addresses all of the above.

The method we will focus on soon in these leadership team meetings is that of instructional practice. First, good instruction has to be defined. Again, that is done by the school community.

Defining Excellence and Seeking It Through Instructional Learning Walks

Deprivatizing practice has been a challenge in most schools for decades (Elmore, 2004). In fact, Elmore indicates that teachers don't have a language to even discuss their practice (Elmore, personal communication, 2010) while Lambert states that they do have a language but are not comfortable having the conversation (Lambert, personal communication, 2011). Whatever the case, many have joked that teaching is the most private of acts in which adults engage!

The CREATE process again turns this inside out, as it is the teachers who first define what they are looking for in good instruction, and then *they* become curious and motivated to find it! Instructional Learning Walks begin with having the leadership team members follow the steps detailed in Tool F.

In the *Tools to Help Answer the Questions in the Room,* there are comprehensive "Steps of Instructional Learning Walks" with questions to facilitate the process in Tool F as well as an "Indicators of Quality Instructional Learning Walks Observation Sheet" in Tool G.

As with all parts of the process described earlier, the leadership/learning team that defines excellence using the previous tool must later redefine it within their larger school community with the other members of that community (more on that in the next chapter). Moreover, once *excellence* is defined, it must be sought within the building to find the positive deviance that exists; but this is not a straight-line process. As described previously, "slow is smooth and smooth is fast," and the effective leadership team will begin on a small scale and with the willing. A detailed case story on how this was done in principal Christine Sermak's Williamston Middle School in Williamston, Michigan, is detailed in Chapter 6.

Once there is clarity around what excellence is being sought, the team will develop a rubric for assessing what they find in their learning walks. Several exist at Answerisintheroom.org. Yet again, going from decades of private teaching with classroom doors closed to having one's instructional approach assessed is not a quick or easy matter. There are many small steps that precede this, demonstrated in case stories in the coming chapters. To close this chapter, let's see what the processes above lead to in terms of teacher engagement and commitment, as described by Sarah Jandrucko, EdD, Area Superintendent, Mansfield Independent School District:

In the beginning, there was a lack of conversation; there definitely was more silence or there may have been one person contributing or the administrators may have been contributing. Teachers on the leadership teams did not speak much. This changed dramatically over time. Teachers began to commit to the process and even take the lead.

Last year and even the beginning of this year, I was thrilled to see a team member who wanted to be the assistant principal at her school. She did not get the job so she remained the reading specialist. I was a little worried because I thought "Is she going to disengage in this team process?" She didn't get the promotion, and have we sort of said, "We don't value you"? I was then blown away by her contribution at the table in her team with the new principal, the same principal that didn't give her the promotion. I think it was because she thought, "I'm a valuable member of this team and the reading specialist; I'm making as much of a contribution as I would if I were assistant principal. Yes I would have loved the job but I'm still a VALUABLE contributing member to this campus."

The ACADEMY moved us from hesitancy to everybody tossing out problem-solving ideas. Sometimes you go into a classroom and you can tell it is not a risk-free environment. When you're in an environment in a classroom where it may be punitive to speak out or to share, you don't get a lot of dialogue. Then you move into a classroom where a teacher has clearly made it a risk-free environment and then you get a lot more dialogue, a lot more willingness to share. I think that's what happened over the 2 to 3 years with the adults in this academy.

It's not that we had been punitive prior, we just didn't have the venue and process for open dialogue. So we moved from, "I'm not sure I can say anything, I'm not sure people are going to act on it, I'm not sure it's going to be valued," to "Oh my goodness, let me toss out this idea." Then somebody would quickly write it down, they might work on it, and it was valued.

As one of the leaders on the steering committee, headed by Superintendent Bob Morrison, Dr. Jandrucko represents an active and fully engaged district leader in this process. Moreover, the entire steering committee supported this approach for 3 years, based on their prior research, the reactions they received from the larger school community prior to beginning, and ongoing assessments of the outcomes of the work. This engagement in, and commitment to, the process was further fueled by their ongoing personal involvement and transparency around plans and results.

THE BIG QUESTION

What is the process, common language, and framework for action that you use across your learning community to *connect the dots* **or bring cohesion to the many initiatives underway?**

The next chapter looks further into processes undertaken to further engage the larger school community in identifying and scaling what is already working in the school community.

An Action Plan for Engaging the Entire Learning Community

"The greatest skill for a school leader is the ability to move adults along, because then the adults are going to move the kids along."

—Ingrid Carney, Past President, Learning Forward

In Chapter 5, leadership groups from the school level came together under the auspices of a committed district steering committee to begin the process of developing real leadership "teams" with a common purpose. They developed common language around their operating protocols and values as well as a common vision for excellence in teaching. This process both put in place foundational and essential aspects of being a high-performing team, and it was done in a manner that fostered trust as an important by-product.

In addition, the process called for use of certain tools that could now be used at the school-building level to mirror the team-building that occurred in the Courageous Leadership Academy (CLA). Some were provided in the last chapter and are in the "Tools to Help Answer the Questions in the Room" in the back of the book. Two other such tools, referenced below, are provided to create SMART goals, and help clarify processes for identifying and refining excellence within the school building.

DEVELOPING A COMMON LANGUAGE FOR THE ACTION PLAN

The tools from the prior chapter would also be among those that these teams draw upon as they are building a more cohesive school culture built on common understandings, transparency, and trust. In the case of the examples provided in this book, the common framework and system for action have been the six principles of *Failure Is Not an Option®*, but others could be used. Sarah Jandrucko, Area Supervisor, explains the importance of having a common framework and language for bringing cohesion to the Mansfield Independent School District, which is now a recognized district in the state of Texas:

We were not a negative district or a dysfunctional district. In fact, we are unusual in that we have no "low-performing" schools. Yet we were a district where most schools are doing their own thing. This was the first time everybody heard the same thing for 3 years; the first time and we gave everybody the same information.

It meant a lot of coordination among our administrators, and as we facilitated, we weren't just sharing the message with administration, we were engaging the teachers, and the teachers in turn were in charge of doing the same with fellow faculty members.

In the past, I think we were much more fragmented. I don't know that we all had the same vocabulary. I don't suppose we had school vertical planning; we had district vertical planning.

Most of the schools were probably independent in the district. And then when we took *Failure Is Not an Option*® and we took those six principles and we began repeating those, and more clearly defining them and grouping all efforts within those principles, it became the common language. That was what we all were beginning to talk about and then that continued on an ongoing basis. We actually asked people to keep their conversations structured to those six principles, because those six principles covered everything that we're about. Some actually structured their school improvement plan to the six principles, but that was only a couple of them.

As mentioned in Chapter 2, another framework might be used in this process, but this is the one we are most familiar with when it comes to doing this district or work. The important thing is that (1) there is a common language; (2) whatever is used be encompassing and providing clarity around virtually all school efforts underway so that cohesion can be created; and (3) the system used is open-ended and neither a prescriptive nor a content-directed program. The framework can then be the overarching umbrella under which specific programs or strategies can be adopted.

Williamston Middle school in Williamston, Michigan, was one of more than 50 schools located within eight districts that undertook this process together with the help of the visionary leadership of Cindy Anderson, Assistant Superintendent of Instruction, Thorburn Education Center. Christine Sermak, the past principal of Williamston, describes how the constructs and new culture they have created are open-ended and oriented toward ongoing learning and improvement:

Now that we have established our core leadership teams, trust has been built and a new way of learning and implementing what we learn is the norm. We have established two groups that help bring a wealth of knowledge into our building. One of them attended a Ken O'Connor session and the other one chose a Carol Commodore training. We've used some of the understanding by design, some of the things that Carol Commodore presented, that teachers are sharing with the staff. Some of the methodologies that are introduced in some of those books are being infused in the teaching.

The foundation for ongoing learning has been laid in this school, beginning with getting the leadership team in synch around critical facets of being a team described earlier. In addition, they have a common language, framework for action, focus on what they want to do, and explicitly planned way of going about learning and infusing that learning throughout the school. Later in this chapter, it becomes clear how this school uses the entire network of eight districts to identify and then adopt positive deviance wherever it is found.

KEY CHALLENGES TO ADDRESS IN THE ACTION PLAN

At the end of each Courageous Leadership Academy (CLA) session, the leadership teams that have met together throughout the district will define the plan for reentry back into their school community, mindful of the perils that likely await! It is often the case that the *transformed* individual or team returns to the prior context and is engulfed once again by the existing culture. As Dennis Sparks pointed out, "Culture trumps innovation" (D. Sparks, personal communication, 2010). It also overrides individuals within that culture—unless there is a plan that takes this into account and a team capable of delivering on that plan.

The latter statement, around "team," versus "individual," is critical to this process. That is the case both in assuring that the group of people in question do in fact become a team as addressed in the prior chapter, and in that this team be representative of the school as a whole (as opposed to reflections only of the leader of that team). Therefore, early and mindful actions are very important to the success of the whole CREATE process. (See sections in Chapter 3, for example, on "Building a Collective Commitment to Scale Up Student Success" and "7 Tools for Constructing a Large-Scale Community Commitment").

The action planning these school leadership teams undertake at the end of each session together is generally around a few key items:

- How will the teams assure transparency with the larger school community they represent?
- How will they engage that community in a fashion similar to how they were engaged in the academy in which all the school teams were convened?*
- What SMART goals will be established to guide their next steps?

REENTRY PLANS TO ENGAGE THE LARGER SCHOOL COMMUNITY, BUILD TRUST, AND ENSURE TRANSPARENCY

Reentry plans are formulated to help school-based leadership teams that are meeting across the district to engage their respective school communities, build trust, and ensure transparency. Assuming the team was well-chosen and has coalesced nicely as a real team, the next step is in how this group will not be redefined by the rest of their

---

*What is the best way for these teams to begin to identify and assess excellence within their school, and affirm common agreement around those practices? What will they bring back to the districtwide CLA meeting of leadership teams to share as artifacts of all the above (Blankstein, 2004/2010)?

school community as *outsiders* of some sort: "Those guys who went to someplace fun while we worked!" The answer comes again in both transparency around what was learned as well as use of the engagement tools and questions—not answers—that are posed of the larger community. In other words, to a great extent the same process that was modeled for the now-developed team will need to be deployed all over again for the school community to get full engagement *and* answers that are pertinent to that particular community.

Thus the values, protocols, purpose, and definition of excellence created by leadership teams and described in prior chapters is not handed from the leadership team to the school staff, but rather *created* together once again. At this point, moreover, the school-based community starts to develop some clear direction for itself, including defining their own SMART goals, and *specific behaviors* that will lead to successful completion of those goals. The implementation of those goals generally begins, as Mel Riddle put it, with the willing and on a small scale. Eventually the use of the entire school district network becomes a major resource for these teams. In the case of Christine Sermak, it went outside of her district to the larger regional network as well:

> In that first year we built relationships with other middle schools. There was time built in during our Academy where we formed relationships with other buildings, so, for example, in that first year we saw a lot of commonalities with Haslett Middle School, which is 15 minutes the road from us. So we sent a team over to see their approach to academic labs for their students who were struggling in literacy and numeracy. We had something very similar, but we said, "Hey we've kind of started it from scratch." So we sent a team of three teachers over there to look at their academic labs to get ideas. We did the same thing with some of their special education classrooms and their resource rooms. So it was really a sharing of ideas as well. Not only was it a celebration of what was already working for them, but we looked at how we could take it to the next level at our building.
>
> We did this with high schools in the network as well. We're looking right now at the idea of going to a skills-based report card. We got the idea from the Holt school district, which was doing that. So I actually contacted their high school principal and he sent over a copy of their report card. It was really collaboration across more than one district.

The above example is what naturally begins to occur when leadership teams (1) use similar relationship-enhancing, trust-building processes to establish their purpose and direction both across the district (or region in this case) and within their schools and (2) develop a common language around core concerns which would include what good instruction looks like and what their common mission, vision, values, and goals (MVVG) are.

DEVELOPING SMART GOALS THAT THE SCHOOL COMMUNITY WANTS TO ACHIEVE

There are several essential considerations in *how* these goals are created, as the process is itself the strategy for success. Although the example of SMART goal development below and the tool for tracking SMART goals are both focused on the *product* of those SMART goals, that product is secondary to how it was derived, who was involved in its creation, how those people were engaged, and how committed to the goal they are.

A context exists in which the school is operating that includes districtwide vision and goals, state and provincial mandates, and so on. Although these must be taken into consideration, the school community itself will define its own priorities if it is willing to do what it takes to succeed in meeting ambitious goals. It is very limiting and demotivating, for example, for a school teacher to have to adhere to testing quotas as her primary focus in life. It may seem even contrary to have that focus for her if she is seeing children on any given day come to school having never had breakfast, or having no permanent home, or being *emotionally* orphaned by two wealthy yet absent parents. None of those *real* life circumstances lead a caring and creative individual to begin the day by calling for those children to sit down and take out their #2 pencil for today's battery of tests.

The practical reader may be groaning at this point. But let's consider a number of ways to meet the *ultimate* aim—at least as it is now defined by one or another test—and yet meet the real needs of our children (as argued prior, the two are inseparable in the long run, in any case; the best way to do poorly on tests is to assure a disengaged, truant student population!).

What if the community started determining its SMART goals in consultation with the students, for example, as Erin Gruwell did as a teacher in Long Beach, California. Her charge was to teach high schoolers literacy through Shakespeare, but she found this gang-affiliated group had only one common interest (survival) and one common story (threatened survival). So she began with *their* story. Once they became interested in and proficient at writing about that story, they eventually became more interested in two other gangs described by Shakespeare: the Montagues and Capulets. Similarly, the example in the section on "Cultivating the Community: Qualities of the Courageous Leader" in Chapter 3 shows how a school community in Clairton, Pennsylvania, realized that the real leverage point for change wasn't around something having to do with "reducing violence," which was rampant, but instead with how the school addressed tardiness—through suspensions—which led students to being angry and out on the streets.

So defining SMART goals in smart ways involves a more comprehensive analysis by the community that will be motivated by and committed to their actualization. Although all this is indeed taken in the context in which we are all operating, that context itself can be distracting not only to doing what is *right,* but even to meeting the goals mandated within that context. In sum, it is the community on the ground, when properly guided and cooperatively engaged, that will most accurately determine both its own problems and the best solutions.

Now for the easy stuff (which is often confused with the *important* stuff)! Here is the definition and example of a SMART goal:

Figure 6.1   Writing an Instructional SMART Goal

A structure and process for writing and monitoring an Instructional SMART Goal

This tool may be used as an exercise to practice developing an Instructional SMART Goal. Once introduced to participants it may be used by School Leaders to develop and monitor Instructional SMART Goals with school faculty.

S =	Specific and Strategic	What specifically are we trying to accomplish? What results do we want? How is it relevant to our mission?
M =	Measurable	What measure will indicate we have accomplished our goal? How can the results be quantified?
A =	Achievable	Is this goal possible to achieve? Is it action-oriented and acceptable? What action steps will we take to achieve it? Are all stakeholders, including our team, in agreement with the goal?
R =	Realistic and Results Oriented	Are there any hindrances that are insurmountable? Is it possible and realistic, within the specified time frame?
T =	Time Bound	When should the goal be completed? Does it have a starting point, ending point, and fixed duration?

Instructional SMART Goal:	
Start date of Instructional SMART Goal:	
Target date for completion of Instructional SMART Goal:	
Results for this goal: How will we know when we have reached it?	

The following Instructional SMART Goal formula is offered as a tool for communicating Instructional SMART Goals:

We will _____ (action verb, object), so that_____ (who and how many) will demonstrate _____ as evidenced by _____ (to what level) by _____ (when).

Example:

We will **improve math achievement**, so that **80% of the fifth-grade students** will demonstrate **math proficiency** as evidenced by **proficient or advanced scores on the April 2010 statewide math test.**

SUCCESSFUL IMPLEMENTATION OF SMART GOALS

Another important feature of effective use of SMART goals is not only their creation but in their implementation. Many people tend to have one of two common reactions to a process that calls for them to learn from positive deviants and change their own behaviors accordingly. One is not to notice the difference between what the other person is doing and what the observer generally does: "We already do that?!" It takes awhile to train oneself to find what is exceptional versus what is already known in a behavior or situation. "Not finding new lands, but seeing with new eyes," as Marcel Proust once wrote. Changing the perspective to that of say a treasure hunter can be helpful. When this was done across one school system, those hunting treasure also looked for museum pieces that were to be honored for what they had accomplished, but not used. They also looked for gold to be used widely, and so on. Changing the rules of the game can shift one's normal vantage point of *discarding* to one that will lead to *discovery*.

The second common obstacle to successful implementation is that of lack of ability or confidence on one's ability. This too may lead one to say, "We are already doing that!" but for different reasons than above. It is also common to hear: "That would never work here!" which again could mean the same thing: "I can't do that."

As demonstrated by Bandura's work helping people overcome their fear of snakes, the level of success in implementation is connected to two things: (1) Does the community creating the goal care a lot about it?; and (2) do they believe they can accomplish it?

Addressing this second point, Bandura's work around *vicarious learning* is again very helpful. Successful leadership teams not only assure goals that people are truly committed to, but also provide models of the new behavior that are accompanied with enough support to assure likely success for the newly initiated. The following case story provides a good illustration of much of this chapter.

Case Story:
SMART Goals—Smart Implementation

After the leadership team from Williamston Middle School had reviewed with the staff their Mission, Vision, and Values, it was time to lock in on one to two core SMART goals. Having goals that are very few in number and eventually get down to the specific *behavioral* changes that will lead to their becoming a reality is key to success.

The school community determined that there were two high-leverage points for making significant gains with their students. One had to do with the whole child. Behaviors that were monitored involved physical and emotional health, and programs that were organically created included "Kick Butts"—a campaign designed to reduce or circumvent smoking.

The second SMART goal was "All students will be proficient in reading and writing in all content areas within 2 years" (this is SMART: **S**pecific and **S**trategic in that it is focused on a high-leveraged area that aligns with their overall plan to assure student success. It is Measurable by the proficiency tests. It is Achievable in their estimation and given a series of SMART tactics, like the one that follows. It is Results oriented, as it focuses on the outcome of their work, although the rest of the work is focused on behaviors that will yield that outcome. It is Time-bound in that they are expecting it to happen within 2 years). There were several clear tactics identified to influence teachers' behaviors toward achieving their goal. One of those tactics was to introduce writing across the curriculum, which would eventually have a common graphic organizer, editing tool, and rubric for assessment (to see all these artifacts, as well as surveys of their community to determine focus areas for their professional development tapping internal expertise, and then translated into common rubrics for learning walks, which were then evaluated using common rubrics, go to Answerisintheroom.org). Christine Sermak and teacher, Laura Hill, describe:

> Sermak: I think that the biggest thing that we've seen goes to our SMART goal about common practices and we've come to that by having our in-services centered around teacher leaders. For example, I and three other language arts teachers came together and asked, "How can we introduce writing across the curriculum for all content areas so it's something that teachers feel comfortable with even if they teach another subject area like math or science?" So what we did is begin with people who would be willing to volunteer. Two science teachers, an art teacher, a Spanish teacher, and a physical education teacher partnered with a language arts teacher, and the teacher helped walk them through a writing assignment using the common graphic organizer that we created and also the common rubric and helped guide them through along the way. And they were kind of our . . . I don't want to say guinea pigs, but our pilot. They kind of ran a pilot, and we introduced that then to the whole staff and had the science teacher or the Spanish teacher talk about their experience of teaching and assessing writing, and that worked extremely well. And that spring-boarded into everyone signing up for a walk-through that would go in and see another teacher teach writing. We even have an e-mail going around, for example, if a teacher's going to teach, like the graphic organizer, other teachers can go into the classroom and then somebody from the main office will come in and act as a substitute for their class so that they can go sit in and see another teacher present it to their class.
>
> So is it the norm now to open your classroom regularly to others. They sign up to go to a class based on what areas they need to know more about in order to excel toward the goal. An e-mail will go out and say: "Hey! I'm teaching this if you want to come in and see it. Find somebody to sub for your class and bop in there."

(Continued)

(Continued)

It became an expectation before December of 2008 that all classrooms would be open to other learners. The trust had been built and the barriers began to be broken down and it wasn't, "I close my classroom door and I'm the only one in there." Now we're working on common assessments there's just so many other avenues that we've opened up. I think the learning walk approach was really was a biggie.

Laura Hill: I've been working with one of our academic lab teachers, who has a really strong knowledge in writing and literacy. We'll get together over lunch, and I'll pick her brain about how to better incorporate the editing tool in my math classroom with my writing and then she'll give me a good idea and I'll say, "Oh how about if we do this in partners?" "Oh I've never tried that! Why don't you try that?" and then she comes in and observes me while I'm teaching and gives me great feedback. And then we send out e-mails to the staff, "Hey, I'm doing this if anyone wants to pop down. This is the time. Come on down, you know, and check it out." And I think this has really opened up our classroom doors and opened up a lot more collaboration among teachers.

The previous case story is a good depiction of the process in action. Beginning with the leadership team in the CLA, common MVVG had been defined, and trust built. Tools like the Instructional Learning Walks (Chapter 5) and SMART goal creation were used first in the CLA with all leadership teams, then practiced, and used again by those leadership teams at the building level to engage their entire learning community. This led to creation of a learning goal around literacy. This goal was made with an eye toward leveraging student outcomes and it, in turn, had high-leverage tactics that focused on necessary behavioral changes to meet that goal. The small-scale launch with the willing volunteers, along with the other foundational groundwork mentioned previously, reduced resistance, and the focus on successes built momentum (see "Commitment" in Chapter 3) for more to adopt the positive deviance (PD) that was underway. Although in this case PD was *created* by those in the pilot, the process is the same as if it is already underway (as was the case in this school's use of the practices already working in other schools within the network, mentioned previously).

IDENTIFYING AND ASSESSING EXCELLENCE

The CREATE process calls for developing means of assessing efforts that are appropriate for what is being assessed and for the developmental stage of the community. So, for example, the initial assessments of the learning walks-in Mansfield described previously were only a quick positive statement or two about what had been seen in the classroom.

The focus was on what was working, and it was far from a rigorous evaluation. This is common in early stages in order to build trust and to focus on what the observer might learn that would be helpful to him.

The tool provided in Chapter 5 to develop a common definition of instructional excellence is introduced early on as well but is not necessarily used formally until the community is prepared for that. Likewise, a more intensive form of individual feedback will come into play at the appropriate time in the school's development. Based on the work of David Allen, Joe McDonald, and others at the Coalition of Essential Schools (CES), for example, *tuning protocols* can be used. They were developed as a way "a teacher presents actual work before a group of thoughtful 'critical friends' in a structured reflective discourse aimed at 'tuning' the work to higher standards" (p. 2, March 1995 edition of "Horace," the publication of CES) (see www.answerisintheroom.org for a version that could be applied to giving and receiving feedback in your school community).

The big SMART literacy goal in Williamston, therefore, was broken down into many smaller SMART tactics, which acted as quick wins for the team. They were constantly measured and cause for celebration, which helped keep everyone on track (remember how the weighing in of children in Vietnam occurred at the end of 6 months to see if the Sternins and Save the Children would be allowed to stay longer? This occurred many times prior to the *final exam,* and each time more families would join the *heavyweights* and celebrate success while the others would redouble their efforts and get additional supports to that end). Each SMART tactic at Williamston—building a common graphic organizer, an editing tool, a common rubric—helped build confidence and trust of the staff involved, as it served as an open invitation for all others to join.

In the SMART goals case study discussed earlier, a very collaborative group that had built trusting relations was able to develop a rubric used early on to evaluate good teaching of writing and literacy across the curriculum. It became a cornerstone of improving their literacy instruction throughout the school, as Christine Sermak describes:

> We've even taken it to the next level in that now we're now as a whole staff looking at student work. We had teachers bring in student work from their classes and put it up on the document camera and everybody is talking about, "Would you give this a 1, 2, 3, or 4 using our common rubric?" So I think again that collaboration has helped us assess writing with a more critical eye. In turn, we're going to at the end of the year, see what our beginning writing looks like that we introduced back in November, and then we'll look at it again in May and see how our students' writing has improved and not rely on our standardized tests, but look at our in-house data.
>
> The main thing is that instead of Lauren going into her classroom and just analyzing her data or her student writing on her own, she's going to sit down with a cross-curricular group of teachers and analyze just a couple of pieces so that again we're all having that common eye as we begin looking at and analyzing the student writing. Then what we'll do is we will look at the data from each classroom and get feedback from teachers as far as how their

students improved or didn't improve—and two of our goals are writing for a purpose as well as editing what we've seen across our building—and see how we've improved on that or where else do we need to put some more emphasis on in our teaching."

Here is a snapshot of the gains of that school over this time period.

Figure 6.2 Gains From Williamston Middle School

Sixth Grade			
% Students Meeting Expectations		Math	Reading
2005		80.80%	89.00%
2006		80.90%	90.10%
2007		85.20%	92.30%
2008		89.40%	94.40%
2009		89.40%	95.60%
Seventh Grade			
% Students Meeting Expectations		Math	Reading
2005		73.50%	91.00%
2006		81.10%	85.10%
2007		83.90%	87.40%
2008		95.00%	90.80%
2009		95.80%	97.20%
Eighth Grade			
% Students Meeting Expectations		Math	Reading
2005		86.40%	88.00%
2006		85.30%	90.20%
2007		88.20%	86.80%
2008		90.90%	83.30%
2009		82.10%	89.40%

THE BIG QUESTION

What tools and processes do your action plans consistently use to assure engagement of and rigorous analysis by the entire learning community? What would it take to use a process like that described in this chapter?

In this chapter, we have looked at how teams beginning with a common system and framework for action, use the processes, tools, and common definitions for excellence to begin to more fully engage their larger school communities. The action planning is done with an explicit focus not on the plan itself, but on the process by which the leadership team engenders commitment to a plan that is important to them. Developing the likelihood of full implementation of these plans and SMART goals has to do with both how salient the goals are to that community and with how likely they feel they are to succeed in accomplishing them.

Starting slow is important to build confidence in the school professionals' ability to succeed, and in building the trust and relationships necessary to sustain that success. This chapter also addressed the more intensive and rigorous kinds of learning across a school, district, or multiple districts that can and naturally will go on when the proper pillars for success are in place. All this is fed by ongoing and increasingly rigorous assessment of instruction by the community itself, regardless of what external evaluations are underway.

The next step for the leadership team is to bring back to the districtwide CLA gathering artifacts of their work in the building so as to expedite learning across the district, region, or province. The next chapter provides a brief overview of this process.

Transference Of Knowledge and Skills Throughout the Learning Community

The history of U.S. Education is certainly littered with the failure of very good ideas to persist even in a single school, much less spread to other schools.

—Karen Seashore Louis

Deep and enduring learning for adults has come as a result of the relationships that have been built in the process.

—Deborah Childs-Bowen

In prior chapters, we laid the foundation for positive deviance to be transferred and scaled throughout the school and network of schools. In this chapter, examples of constructs that facilitate that transfer are profiled. The means by which good practice is scaled vary somewhat from one school and district to another. Decisions around which particular knowledge and skills are transferred, moreover, are totally a function of each community's priorities, as outlined in previous chapters. Since the committed community (see Chapter 3) is actively and passionately engaged in continually improving, the practices that are transferred are always changing—each building upon prior knowledge and each meeting the current need of the students and school community.

For decades educators have grappled with the *gee-whiz* effect of watching greatness occur in a school across the street, yet being unable to reproduce it. We struggled even with replicating best practices from one classroom to another, and misdiagnosed the reason for that failure as being the practitioner's *fault*. Policymakers and major corporations responded with more mandates and *teacher-proof* programs, respectively, and professionals and students in turn disengaged.

In contrast, the preceding chapters call for a new, inside-out approach to fully engaging the entire learning community in defining what is important to *them*. Then, the community is able to identify and find excellence. This chapter focuses on leveraging the expertise within that community to scale that excellence throughout the district, region, province, or (conceivably) state. Effectively using the techniques following, therefore, rests on creation of the conditions outlined in prior chapters. Once those conditions exist, transference and scaling of good practice is achievable and each iteration of transferring good practice begins to act as a flywheel, increasing speed and frequency of the scaling process as time goes on.

Following is Part 1 of a case story demonstrating how it works.

TRANSFERRING KNOWLEDGE AND SKILLS WITHIN THE SCHOOL

**Case Story Part 1:
Rogene Worley Middle School Transfers Positive Deviance in the Building to Lower Suspensions**

Three years ago, Rogene Worley Middle School was experiencing some 4,500 referrals to the principal's office annually, leading to a large number of school suspensions and detentions among its 850 students. After having joined the

(Continued)

(Continued)

district initiative focused on the CREATE process, the school community used its growing levels of trust, communication skills, and learning walk protocols to tackle discipline. They honed in on those teachers who had success with the same students with whom others were experiencing problems. A group of teachers, including some from the leadership team, used their instructional learning walk protocols (Chapter 4) to observe what those successful teachers did in their interactions with students who were frequently sent by other teachers to the principal's office.

The search for positive deviance within the school revealed that although some teachers would call a lot of attention to a minor infraction (like throwing a pencil), other more successful teachers would deal with such incidents by quietly approaching the student, indicating that the behavior was not in concert with required class behavior, and ask, "Are you having a problem with the lesson?" The answer was often "yes," and the behavior was caused by student frustration over not understanding the lesson.

These very specific behaviors of not escalating the problem, speaking quietly with the student to correct the behavior, and inquiring about the cause were among those that the team locked in on as being effective and transferable. There were others as well. They included developing engaging curriculum and teaching strategies that were relevant to students. Strategies for building relationships with students on the front end of the school year were also identified.

Once the successful behaviors of positive deviants had been identified, the next step was to transfer or normalize that throughout the school. This school had been working on the CREATE process long enough to have already built the infrastructure and culture necessary to do this. In their case they had a sophisticated structure for meeting, discussing, and acting on positive practices found within the building, as outlined below in Part 2 of this case story.

The outcome for this school is that it cut its referrals by 50% in 2 years, and cut its obligatory summer school attendance by two thirds in the same time period.

In addition to the reduction in discipline referrals, the flywheel went into effect. They furthered their collaborative culture built on trust and the concept that everyone had ownership in the success of the campus. This gave teachers a new passion for sharing their good practices to ensure student success, thus increasing student engagement in the classrooms while also decreasing the number of discipline referrals.

The previous case demonstrates some important features of the process of transferring and scaling good practices of outliers to make these practices the norm:

1. The problem identification began with hard and soft data around large numbers of students being disciplined.

2. The school community decided this was important to them. This was not prioritized for them externally.

3. The group that identified the problem was the group *with* the problem *and* the solution.

4. The ability for practitioners to research effective internal solutions was founded on prior work through the process outlined in the preceding chapters. Walking into a teacher's room cold and looking for the answer to this problem would not have been effective. Even if the answer had been found, there would have been resistance to acting on it systemwide.

5. The outlier behaviors found were depersonalized and analyzed separate from the teachers displaying them. The answer was not to change the teacher, but to discover the effective *method* and share that with *all* other teachers.

6. The successful *behaviors* or teaching *methods* were isolated and taught widely throughout the school, leading to changed outcomes for the entire school.

This approach to finding, transferring, and scaling good practice is far different than brining in a program such as "You Name It Discipline!" That is because (1) it provides a solution that is already working within the context in which the problem is found; (2) since it is already working in that context, this approach would have more credibility and be more likely to be adopted by others; and (3) the successful behaviors are not clouded or packaged along with other less pertinent strategies. Rather, they are very specific to the needs in this context and of this community.

The structures that allow for the school community to identify, share, and then implement systemwide the new practices will vary significantly. Each community has its own set of possibilities and constraints to consider. Here is how Rogene Worley Middle School typically normalizes good practices such as those found in the previous case story.

Case Story Part 2:
Rogene Worley Middle School Structures for Scaling Success

The school does professional development every day for 85 minutes. Monday, Wednesday, and Friday, they meet in their interdisciplinary clusters composed of four core subject-area teachers, and four to six elective-area teachers and support staff. On Tuesday and Thursday, they meet peers within the same discipline area, such as seventh-grade math. The school has two interdisciplinary

(Continued)

(Continued)

teaching teams per grade level (so for seventh grade, there are the Cheetahs and the Jaguars). The school uses a block schedule approach, and students are taking electives while teachers are in their daily 85-minute professional development.

The staff was once reluctant to open their doors to another teacher. They built trust and commitment to this through approaches described in earlier chapters, including having the idea initially presented by peers (who also happened to be on the Courageous Leadership Academy [CLA] leadership teams); starting in a nonevaluative manner with volunteers; providing only structured, brief, and positive feedback initially; and modeling the process and positive outcomes to get larger participation. It took almost a year for more rigorous and evaluative feedback to be used during the learning walks.

Now the staff is hungry to constantly learn from one another. Once a new successful practice is discovered, several things occur. The practice comes to the attention of the leadership team as well as the vertical and content-specific teams. Depending on where it is most applicable, it will become an agenda item for demonstration in one of the daily meetings. From that point, it will not only be observed, but also practiced in the pertinent meeting. Members of that team will commit to actions relative to using the new practice in their respective classrooms. They will then report back to the team and/or entire school staff (in the case of reducing discipline referrals schoolwide, for example) as to what the results were. The team will then determine next steps together, which may include additional support for one member, sharing more widely the new practice, or modifying the practice according to new information on how to improve upon it.

The structure for scaling excellence above is well-defined and well-financed. In the case of the Renaissance Middle School in Queens, New York, Principal Harriett Diaz has established another system for continuously seeking and scaling good practice.

To get from almost being closed down (see Chapter 1) to being rated an "A" school by the New York Board of Education, they decided early on that they would restructure their large student body into four smaller mini-schools focused on different academic pursuits, yet literacy-rich classrooms would be a common theme across all four.

One teacher purchased an inexpensive lounge chair and brought it into her classroom, creating a living room where she does her read-alouds with her students. This is not normal for middle schools, so other teachers needed to see it to not only believe it but to try it. Twice a month the staff gathers for such embedded learning experiences, and this teacher's classroom was the site for one gathering. Other staff and parents were also able to see displays on the bulletin board of developmental stages of her students—writing from "draft" to "work in progress" to "completion" highlight steps—all on the bulletin board. This was a technique to help all have clarity and students work harder using these tangible examples of their own work.

These practices were discussed, leading to some others trying them. The results of some staff using the approach led to more of the same, until it became the norm for the school.

TRANSFERRING KNOWLEDGE AND SKILLS THROUGHOUT THE DISTRICT

The transference of skills and knowledge goes in many directions once the district and schools are aligned. In the case of this district, Mansfield Independent School District (ISD), the area superintendents are actively engaged in the process as well. They each spend *a minimum of* 3½ days in the schools each week. They act as learners looking for excellent practices, coaches, and mentors. They use a "Campus Visit Protocol" (Available at the www.answerisintheroom.org website) that they all have agreed upon and a common language for understanding and acting on what they see and learn.

Each week the area superintendents meet, and once a month they have a sharing out on what is working at the building sites. This is one of several ways they scale successful practices districtwide. Another way is through an ad hoc meeting like one that was designed to scale a practice that math teachers could all benefit from. For this they brought 50 math teachers together for an entire day in which they learned the practice and then embedded it into their lessons for the subsequent 6 weeks. The day-long session was led by the teachers who understood and were using the practice.

Sarah Jandrucko, Area Superintendent at Mansfield ISD, explains:

> We had the math teachers across the district get together, their principals supported them, they spent one day developing 21 exemplary lessons in their content area. Their facilitator was a math teacher in the district.
>
> We had to giggle because our math content coordinator didn't do it, a *teacher* did it. And the principal brought that teacher to one of our principals' meetings so the teacher could demonstrate some things he'd done, and everybody looked at him and said, "Wouldn't this be good for other teachers?" and he said, "Of course it would. I'll organize it for you." And then the teacher just volunteered to organize it.
>
> Those teachers will take that back, and the students across this district will have commonly planned exceptionally good lessons. And that came from those teachers. Now we're starting to see lots of teachers and lots of people together in a collaborative style; the teachers are coming together to write curriculum. They say, "We want to get together." The math teachers say this! We must have
>
> *(Continued)*

(Continued)

had 50 teachers in the room—Algebra 1 and Geometry, Algebra II, and I think our pre-Calculus teachers. And so they were sitting in their content area working with teachers from all four high schools developing lessons together.

Now all four high schools are going to use the same solid lessons built on standards that came out of a drive by teachers. They now know that's acceptable; that's what we expect. Now they're taking on and saying, "Well, let's get Algebra 1 teachers together so we can talk and plan together." So, now the teachers are doing that—they're talking about prevention, intervention, and good lessons, and we want good lessons so kids don't fail.

Another means of scaling positive practices is through a mechanism such as the CLA, which brings together school and district leadership teams four times a year. Each session begins with following up on the commitments for action made at the prior session, and teams share with one another artifacts of what they have done and what they have learned from it. The Rogene Worley Middle School, for example, conceded having minimal parental engagement early on, yet getting scores of useful strategies that they implemented from other teams throughout the district. After their first year of focus on this, they tripled parental engagement in school-based activities.

It is common in most districts in North America to have meetings in which information is conveyed. Each month there may be a list of announcements that the superintendent wants to convey, for example. There may even be the same format available to principals or teachers to share out something important, including best practices underway, or something recently learned in a workshop offsite. In addition, in-service days and back-to-school kick-offs have a valid ritualistic place in the life of the school community and are a regular feature.

What is relatively rare in most districts, however, is a structured process in which participants are using advanced facilitative tools to converse with one another in small groups around what is working, practicing their use of those tools real time, and then committing to specific actions at their school site. When all this is rooted in common mission, values, and goals focusing on critical concerns of the school community, the outcomes are powerful.

TUNING PROTOCOL

A Tool to Refine Practice Making PD the Norm

A *tuning protocol* is a staff-development process that is embedded in what a teacher does in the classroom or what an educator does in a school. A group of colleagues come together to examine each other's work, honor the good things found in that work, and fine-tune it through a formal process of presentation and reflection (Easton, 1999).

Tuning protocols provide a structure and process for professional dialogue to learn from our work. This process helps fine-tune educational practices using a *protocol* or formal process for examining our work in a supportive, problem-solving group. Four reasons to use tuning protocols, including the following:

1. *Tunings provide accountability beyond test scores.* We need to get different information from different kinds of data, not just comparisons against a population (norm-reference tests) or comparison to a standard (criterion-reference tests). We need a repertoire. We also need a source of data that is less invasive than a test.

2. *Tunings provide information useful in a classroom.* By looking directly at student work, we learn what students really know and can do in the context of their real work—and why. We also learn what students do not know and cannot do. These are important insights for anyone educating young people.

3. *Tunings build a learning community.* They are content rich since they focus on student work and educator practice. For these reasons, they ensure some level of application.

4. *Tunings work.* The process is relatively risk-free, and the results are richer than those from a typical discussion. Most importantly, everybody learns from a tuning protocol. The tuning protocol allows everyone to think deeply about student work and educator practice, arrive at creative solutions, and connect with colleagues (Easton, 2008).

Figure 7.1   Tuning Protocols Do's and Don'ts: Critical Aspects of Doing a Tuning on Your Own

- ❑ Tuning protocols work best if participants and presenters think of their work as a collaboration to help students learn.

- ❑ Be vigilant about keeping time. Be sure to work through the entire protocol for the process to be effective. Do not let one person monopolize any part of the protocol.

- ❑ Try to gather the same group each time a protocol is done.

- ❑ If presenters come from within a group of people who will, themselves, do a protocol, they'll feel a little less intimidated about sharing the work they and/or their students are doing.

- ❑ The group should be somewhat protective of the presenter—by making their work public, presenters expose themselves to a critique.

- ❑ The room facilitator should help participants recast or withdraw inappropriate comments.

(Continued)

Figure 7.1 (Continued)

> ❑ The room facilitator can also ask how "tough" the presenter wants participants to be.
>
> ❑ Participants should also be courteous, thoughtful, and provocative. Be provocative of substantive discourse. Many presenters may be used to blanket praise. Without thoughtful but probing cool questions and comments, they won't benefit from the tuning protocol experience. Presenters often say they'd have liked more cool feedback (Cushman, 1995).
>
> ❑ Consider having an outside facilitator who does not participate in the process, at least for the first tuning.
>
> ❑ The facilitator should make sure all steps are followed, keep time, be sure that the group acts according to the assumptions, monitor airtime, check for the balance of warm and cool feedback, and make sure the group addresses the presenter's key questions. Without a facilitator, consider having participants take on these roles.

Warm and Cool Feedback

Joe McDonald, Coalition of Essential Schools, uses the terms *warm* and *cool feedback*. Nothing is gained if participants only praise, but praise should be part of a protocol. What worked? Nothing is gained if participants only criticize, but a critique should be part of a protocol. What would help students learn better?

- *Warm feedback* consists of statements that let the presenter know what is working. Warm feedback takes the form of praise for what seems effective.
- *Cool feedback* consists of statements or questions that help the presenter move forward. They are less criticism than a critique of the work. They are oriented to improving the work and the work context. Cool feedback is never about the presenter—only about what the presenter brought to be tuned. The best cool feedback occurs through "What if . . ." questions such as, "I wonder what would happen if . . ." (Easton, 2008).

When the Rogene Worley leadership team learned about tuning protocols (see Case Story 1), for example, they practiced their use in front of one another and then again with feedback from other peers in the cohort during the CLA session. After that, they filmed themselves using the protocols and shared that film with their larger school community when they returned. In addition, they demonstrated use of the protocols live with their staff and allowed the rest of the teachers to practice using them as well. This went on both in staff meetings and eventually in classrooms over the following 6 weeks. Ultimately, this tool became a regular part of the culture, which has allowed for a more powerful approach to their learning walks. When they returned to the CLA for the next session, they had much to share, including some new actors in their videos!

THE BIG QUESTION

This chapter has been about scaling good or excellent practice within a school or throughout a school district. To date, this has arguably been, along with sustainability, among the holy grails in education. Our experience indicates that this has not been because of a lack of effort, nor lazy, inept or otherwise bad educators. It has been because of a lack of good methodology. If one tries to scale success by using past methods, it will likely not succeed any better than has been the case for the past century. The successful spreading of excellence requires many preliminary steps described in prior chapters. The good news is it is achievable! This chapter shared not only the process, but many examples of success. The next chapter will focus on embedding both the successful new practices and the processes for continually discovering and scaling them.

Embedding the New Learning in the Culture for Sustainability

"*The kind of high-intensity, job-embedded collaborative learning that is most effective is not a common feature of professional development across most states, districts, and schools in the United States.*"

—Stephanie Hirsh

"Ultimately a school's culture has far more influence on life and learning in the schoolhouse than the state department of education, the superintendent, the school board, or even the principal can ever have."

—Roland Barth (2001)

T he overarching focus of the CREATE process has been around developing the critical, job-embedded, sustained and intensive adult-learning that leads to student achievement gains (Darling-Hammond et al., 2009). The process leads to courageous instructional leaders at all levels who design, implement, monitor, and improve classroom instruction (Louis et al., 2010). There is a strong correlation between implementation of this process and student achievement (American Institutes for Research, 2011). The question now becomes how to embed and sustain the new practices in the new culture they have helped to engender. Shaping the culture is one of the most critical jobs for the school and district leader (Deal & Peterson, 2009; Schien, 2004; D. Sparks and J. Klien, personal communication, 2010).

Deal and Peterson put this into perspective:

A great deal of attention has been paid to making schools better. Policymakers want to get schools to change quickly and be more responsive to state mandates. The favored response has been to tighten up structures, standardize the curriculum, test student performance, and make schools accountable. In the short term, these solutions may pressure schools to change some practices and temporarily raise test scores. In the long term, such structural demands can never rival the power of cultural expectations, motivations and values. (2009, p. x)

Without an explicit focus on this aspect of schooling, everything covered in the prior chapters will dissipate after the next major funding cycle, new state or provincial mandate, or shift in leadership. By contrast, schools that have laid the proper groundwork throughout each phase of the process have endured major shifts in leadership, budget cuts, and reorganization. An example would be Ingham Intermediate School District:

Christine Sermak was the principal of Williamston Middle School, one of scores of schools across eight districts in Michigan that went through much of the CREATE process before the auto industry plummeted, sending this part of the country into double-digit unemployment and fiscal crisis. The positive deviance effort was cut short prematurely. Yet that school, like many others, was able to advance because of the committed culture that had been created. Now Sermak is the principal of Okemus High School, one of the schools in the network she used to partner with during the CREATE process. Even without her at the helm, the middle school maintains much of the culture as is explained by her successor, Scott Martin:

Walk-throughs are not happening consistently anymore. In lieu of that, teachers watch others model a lesson using flip videos in the building. These lessons are shared at faculty meetings and analyzed together using the CUPS rubric we developed (Capitalization; Understanding; Punctuation; Spelling). The S-W-B-A-T (Students Will Be Able To . . .) written planner is also still used to help everyone focus on what students should know at the end of each class period.

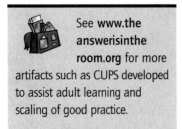

See www.the answerisinthe room.org for more artifacts such as CUPS developed to assist adult learning and scaling of good practice.

Note a few key points here:

1. The school networking led to a transition of leadership in which the middle school principal went to a high school she had already been working with. In addition, she is still associated through a more informal network with the middle school she once headed. Structures shifted, but relationships formed during the Academy, and students at both schools were the beneficiaries. (See Williamston student achievement scores following.)

2. The original structure to support walk-throughs had been dismantled because of budget constraints, yet the intent and outcomes were maintained by the team's development of an alternative. Culture trumps structure.

3. Artifacts of the work of the original interdisciplinary literacy team (see Chapter 5), were intact and useful to help teachers continually improve practice. The results of having a strong culture that embedded the CREATE process can be seen in Figure 8.1.

Figure 8.1 Percentage of Students Meeting Expectations at Williamston Middle School

Sixth Grade			
% Students Meeting Expectations		Math	Reading
2005		80.80%	89.00%
2006		80.90%	90.10%
2007		85.20%	92.30%
2008		89.40%	94.40%
2009		89.40%	95.60%
Seventh Grade			
% Students Meeting Expectations		Math	Reading
2005		73.50%	91.00%
2006		81.10%	85.10%
2007		83.90%	87.40%
2008		95.00%	90.80%
2009		95.80%	97.20%
Eighth Grade			
% Students Meeting Expectations		Math	Reading
2005		86.40%	88.00%
2006		85.30%	90.20%
2007		88.20%	86.80%
2008		90.90%	83.30%
2009		82.10%	89.40%

Given all the challenges inherent in our system of education and articulated in prior chapters (focus on programs vs. process; ever-changing funding streams that support diametrically opposing initiatives, rapid shifts in leadership, and so on), it is a wonder that anything might be sustainable in our field. Billions of dollars are spent in education on throwing out *entire* approaches to school reform, for example, because they are only *partially* effective, and then moving full steam ahead to the next hot reform (Payne, 2010).

Yet, our experience as well as others' research indicates that focus on developing leadership capacity (Leithwood, Harris, & Strauss, 2010) to in turn build the kind of community suggested in prior chapters, connected to a robust learning network of schools, offers the best hope for sustained success (Fullan, 2010; Sharratt & Fullan, 2009; Hargreaves and Shirley, 2009). Embedding in the school culture the CREATE process and many of the protocols and practices it yields is the focus of the rest of this chapter.

THREE PILLARS OF EMBEDDING THE PROCESS IN THE SCHOOL CULTURE

The advantage of having a strong capacity and community building process is that it acts as a flywheel in accelerating adoption of new initiatives deemed worthy of the community. It is like laying down tracks that many trains can glide along, assuming those tracks are well rooted in the ground and regularly maintained. With this in mind, there are three

Figure 8.2 The CREATE Process: Three Pillars

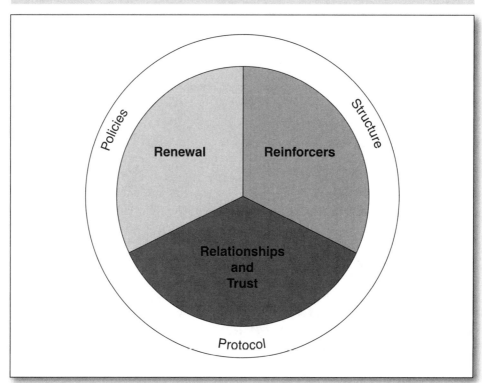

categories of activity to consider when embedding CREATE or any other process in your school culture: Reinforcers; Relationships and Trust; and Renewal. These three Rs often overlap and are ultimately supported in turn by structures, protocols, and policies, as indicated in Figure 8.2.

Reinforcing

In Jackie Robinson Elementary School, a different student welcomes everyone back to school over the loudspeaker each morning. The uplifting announcements include a reflection or poem or other expression connected to the virtue the school is focused on that month in their development of character. At the end, that student and all others listening recite this poem:

The Jackie Robinson School Creed©

The late Jackie Robinson was an extraordinary man.

I live my life knowing that like him, I certainly can.

I can do all things, be all things, and create all things.

I will yearn each day for more and more knowledge.

My dreams will include going to college.

Today, I will respect myself, my teachers, and other boys and girls.

I will live up to my fullest potential to leave my mark in this world.

Success and being the best are the sources of my inspiration,

Because in my heart I know that *Excellence is my only option!*

Written by: Principal Marion Wilson. Used with permission by the HOPE Foundation.

This is one of many rituals that help to build this community and reinforce its commitment to success. Although this particular ritual doesn't focus on the process of scaling positive deviance, as do others below, it does illustrate two elements that are key to reinforcing behaviors: Repetition and Routine.

In Chapter 7, the Rogene Worley Middle school used repetition in assuring quality and consistent implementation of its newly enacted learning walks protocols. The key here was that *everyone* in the community practiced the new technique first in front of peers who eventually gave warm and cool feedback, and then in real classrooms. The leadership team modeled the technique first and even filmed it for peer evaluation and discussion, thereby making it safe to do so for others.

Eventually, after the above repetition, the use of protocols became routine. From that point forward, it was "just the way we do things here."

This process was systematically replicated afterwards. All the principals in the district and their leadership teams shared the positive deviance going on in Worley and other schools and eventually came about standardizing that practice.

The repetition that became routine in one school and replicated in others was also replicated by the district. As shared in the prior chapter, there was a supra-learning team acting as honeybees spreading pollination throughout the district by constantly seeking and sharing positive deviance they encountered (i.e., the 50 math teachers gathering to learn). This approach, in turn, was enhanced through a new policy indicating that all district leaders would spend at least 3½ days a week on campuses as well as structures like their monthly meetings focused on sharing and scaling success.

Rituals help reinforce what is valued in the school and should be explicitly tied to the mission, values, and goals. The worksheet below will help assure this cohesion.

There are many tools available to reinforce the school culture, student learning, or the CREATE process itself:

- Artifacts developed act as visual depictions of what should be reinforced, or tools to advance learning.
- Stories are powerful transmitters and reinforcers of values. In Mali, West Africa, griots are hired privately and supported by the government to recount through song and word centuries of social history at ceremonies, weddings, and other gatherings. They serve to maintain the fabric of that society. Who does this for your school? Is it nurtured explicitly, or is it done by default? If the latter, are the stories ones that uplift and build a positive culture?
- Mottos, aphorisms, and metaphors are all powerful tools for reinforcing what is important. Back to the southern part of Mali, there is a Bambara expression that translates: If you meet five people, three will be friends and two will be relatives. It turns out that generally with enough investigation, the six degrees of separation are collapsed into none in that country—everyone *is* related in some way. Yet, even if that did not turn out to be the case, imagine what this metaphor would convey! No doubt this contributes to why there is so little violence and crime there. Who would rob their friends and relatives?

> See **www.the answerisinthe room.org** for more artifacts such as CUPS developed to assist adult learning and scaling of good practice

Relationships and Trust

Relationships and trust are the lifeblood of the school community (Bryk et al., 2010) and of the school culture. Sustaining and embedding the work that has been done in a school community has a lot to do with depth (How deeply connected are those affected?) and breadth (Is this owned by a small group or the entire community?) (Hargreaves, 2005). The good thing about the CREATE process is that it is by definition rooted in what is of greatest importance to a school community (depth). And, the process for scaling positive deviance is by design inclusive of the entire learning community (breadth).

As pointed out in prior chapters, trusting relations tend to form naturally and positively assuming a well-facilitated process, including good protocols and focused dialogue around areas that are of personal and collective importance in that community. This begins with the leader asking a question, rather than proclaiming a new direction.

When the community is highly distrusting, the questions posed of it are very specific and few in number. In Chapter 3, for example, Harriett Diaz simply asked her staff why they got into the profession in the first place. She synthesized their responses, and provided something they could all agree upon, which was posted throughout the school.

As trust is built, people are focused on working together to solve a problem they have collectively identified as important. This, too, helps foster relationships and trust. When steps toward a solution are identified, they are perused with volunteers first. Support from the leadership in this process further builds relationships, and celebrating small victories helps to gain momentum (discussed in Chapter 3) and trust not only in the person, but in the likelihood of future successes. The monthly contest tied to the mission, vision, values, and goals (MVVG) at Jackie Robinson Elementary school described in Chapter 2 highlights this cycle of engaging peers in their own self-evaluation and celebrating success.

So far, this all is reinforcing of embedding the new initiative process, in the culture. Sounds easy enough, right? We all know that it's easier to get along on a smooth path, but that bumps are inevitable. They usually occur over someone's inability to do the work, lack of clarity around what needs to be done and how to do it; poorly constructed protocols for having a professional conversation; or diverging values.

Trust Built on Truth

I had been looking at grade-level data at the end of quarter two. I have three sections of kindergarten, and one classroom was not moving as I knew they could. I got the three grade levels' data sheets and marked out the teachers' names and asked for a meeting with the grade-level team.

Previously, we discussed sharing lessons, data, asking for help from our in-house resources in staff meetings. We had talked of shared models, peer mentoring, and precision planning of lessons through the use of data in collaboration. Still, this teacher was not moving forward as I had expected her to. As she and I sat in my office and discussed the grade-level data sheets, she noticed that one classroom was not performing as the others had. She noticed the trends, identifying factors, and lack of growth in areas where growth is expected, relative to the amount of growth she had seen in the other two classes. She looked at me, smiled, and asked, "What is this teacher doing?"

I replied, "You tell me." Then she knew it was her class. She felt as though she had cheated her students. From that day forward, she was no longer closed off from outside help. She was a regular contributor to collaboration. We saw a fire that I, in my short time here, had not been seen to date. She had fired herself and hired a new self. I had a brand-new kindergarten teacher from that day forward.

She felt terrible about what she had done.... She never intended to let her students slide under the radar.

Source: Used with permission of Shawn Smiley.

Willard Shambaugh Elementary School, whose principal is Shawn Smiley, was one of the six schools that entered the Courageous Leadership Academy as a beta test, resulting in all 53 (now 51) Fort Wayne Community Schools participating. When Mr. Smiley is confronted with needing to help a staff member improve, he uses it as an opportunity to both build capacity and the relationship.

Mr. Smiley uses a patient, yet urgent approach to changing problematic behavior. Mr. Smiley does not assume bad will or intention on the part of a struggling staff member, and this is where the patience comes in. The process described in this book provides tools for giving feedback and for conversing with colleagues that minimize fallout from conflicts by addressing them productively. It is often the case that lack of capacity, for example, will lead both children and adults to opt out ("This will never work here!"), or to misbehave. Adults as well as children often would rather be good at something that is bad or not working, than be seen as bad at doing something that is good. The antidote for this is also built into the CREATE process, which is all about developing safe spaces for building capacity, starting slow and in a nonevaluative way, and scaling up student success.

When trust and relationships are strong, people become committed to far more than the new initiative. They commit to one another. This is more binding and sustaining than anything else that an organization can offer. Imagine this. Your flight and every other flight to Chicago are cancelled because of a blizzard. Under which of these circumstances are you most likely to rent a car and drive 6 hours to be there? (1) To lead a new teaching technique? (2) To administer a state test? (3) To help a sick friend?

When all else fails, like, for example, the funding dries up, the state issues a new mandate to change direction, or the schools become amalgamated, it will be the relationships that endure. And they will inspire you to greater heights.

Renewal

Renewal comes in several forms. Optimizing energy levels on a daily basis is important. For example, most creative work is usually best done in the morning, whereas many administrative tasks can be handled when one's energy is waning. In addition, marathon-like work schedules are not as productive as is one organized as a series of sprints with regular breaks throughout the day (Loehr & Schwartz, 2003).

Renewal also comes from having internal feedback loops that tell you and the team how you are doing. Although this is often in the form of hard data on test scores, attendance, student engagement, and the like, the qualitative data are at least as important. Consider this story, again, from Shambaugh Elementary:

> The little girl made her way to the principal's office again, but this time she started the conversation:
> "I know Mr. Smiley, I am here because I was angry in class! I'm sorry. I just can't control myself sometimes. It's like that at home, too. Sometimes I think I should just run away from home!"
> Mr. Smiley: "Well, why don't you run away from home?"
> Girl: "Because you guys would miss me here. And I would miss you. I know what you're doing here—now I see teachers talking to each other all the time about how to make things better for us. And I want to be a part of that!"

Imagine how renewing this *story* must be for that school community. The reality of this little girl's story would far surpass seeing on a piece of paper that an anonymous student went from below to above proficiency. It is indeed the stories, their repeated telling, that help to root people in the culture while renewing their energy for continuing the climb.

Renewal comes also from closing the circle on the learning. When teachers step up and organize on their own professional development for their peers, as one high school math teacher did for 50 others in Mansfield (see Chapter 7), then the cycle is complete. Peers are formally and informally renewing one another's commitment and motivation. One teacher summarized: "We used to do what we were told. Now we help run the school."

The inside loops of qualitative and quantitative feedback as well as internally driven and embedded staff development lay the foundation for learning and assimilating ideas from outside the community as well. Although there is tremendous expertise within the district, there are lessons to be learned beyond it. Taking time to do this and then integrating and adapting those lessons internally can be very energizing, especially when the lessons are driven by a particular need the community has identified as important.

Finally, embedding the CREATE or any other process into the culture will take into account transitions and new hires. Developing a good process for assuring new hires are aligned with the values of the community is essential. In the case of Renaissance Middle School in Queens, New York, for example, a new teaching applicant will go through five interviews with staff at all levels and even parents before sealing the deal! The last interview calls for the prospective teaching to demonstrate a sample lesson, and the audience includes both the principal, Harriett Diaz, and some of her students. After the lesson, Harriett will ask her students: "Do you think you could learn from this teacher?"

THE BIG QUESTION

Harriett Diaz's students know that they count as does her larger internal and external school community. When she first showed up for the job, they didn't even expect to see her another day. She's now been there for years, and no one doubts her any longer. Nor do they doubt themselves. They found out early on that even though they were a failing school, they actually did have the answer. What they lacked was someone who would ask them the right questions, listen to them, believe in them, organize the school accordingly, and act on those answers . . . and then do it all again. Just before the cut scores changed dramatically last year, Renaissance Middle School was given an "A" rating by the New York Board of Education. Yet they now have an embedded process, capacity, and commitment necessary to tackle any challenge, and they are confident they will quickly go from their current B back to A rating.

The idea that the answer is in the room is no longer in question for a growing number of enlightened reformers, practitioners, and researchers. Until recently, we were all perplexed as to why it didn't just naturally travel out of the classroom, down the hallway, over to the next building, and throughout the region. Wouldn't seeing a better mousetrap be enough to make you build one, too?!

Now we have the answer. It's a series of questions beginning with: What matters most to you? If we can connect with that, we can use a process like CREATE to make that dream a reality. The big question to you the reader is what matters most to *you?* You can join your peers in working through that as well as taking a self-assessment on your readiness to CREATE the possible at Answerisintheroom.org.

There has never been a more critical point for us to make a difference. I wish you Godspeed in that!

Tools to Help Answer the Questions in the Room

A structure and process for writing and monitoring an Instructional SMART Goal

This tool may be used as an exercise to practice developing an Instructional SMART Goal. Once introduced to participants, it may be used by School Leaders to develop and monitor Instructional SMART Goals with school faculty.

S =	Specific and Strategic	What specifically are we trying to accomplish? What results do we want? How is it relevant to our mission?
M =	Measurable	What measure will indicate we have accomplished our goal? How can the results be quantified?
A =	Achievable	Is this goal possible to achieve? Is it action-oriented and acceptable? What action steps will we take to achieve it? Are all stakeholders, including our Team, in agreement with the goal?
R =	Realistic and Results Oriented	Are there any hindrances that are insurmountable? Is it possible and realistic, within the specified time frame?
T =	Time Bound	When should the goal be completed? Does it have a starting point, ending point, and fixed duration?

Instructional SMART Goal:	
Start date of Instructional SMART Goal:	
Target date for completion of Instructional SMART Goal:	
Results for this goal: How will we know when we have reached it?	

The following Instructional SMART Goal formula is offered as a tool for communicating Instructional SMART Goals:

We will _____ (action verb, object), so that_____ (who and how many) will demonstrate _____ as evidenced by _____ (to what level) by _____ (when).

Example:

We will **improve math achievement**, so that **80% of the fifth-grade students** will demonstrate **math proficiency** as evidenced by **proficient or advanced scores on the April 2010 statewide math test.**

TOOL B: STRATEGIES FOR MAKING TIME

❑ Share classrooms. Plan and schedule team teaching and multidisciplinary class time.

❑ Adjust daily schedule. Teachers agree to arrive sufficiently in advance of classes starting to allow for meeting time. Classes can also be started late one day a week to add 15 to 20 extra minutes to regular early meeting time.

❑ Bring classes together. Have classes exchange visits on a reciprocal basis (e.g., fifth graders visit first-grade classes to read or work with younger children, and first graders visit fifth graders on alternate weeks) and be supervised by one teacher, freeing up the other one.

❑ Use assemblies to free up time. Schedule buildingwide or schoolwide events (movies, assemblies, and so on) during which classroom teachers can meet while students are supervised by counselors, paraprofessionals, or administrators.

❑ Give common assignments. Several classrooms of students at the same grade level (or taking the same course) are given the same assignment or project simultaneously.

❑ Videos, library time, or other related activities are scheduled for all the classes at once, freeing their teachers to meet together while aides, volunteers, or others supervise.

❑ Use parent or business volunteers. Involve parents as aides or chaperones for appropriate activities. Invite local business representatives to share their particular expertise as they supervise classes.

❑ Free up the fifth day. Schedule all academic classes to take place four days each week, leaving the fifth day free for team meetings while students rotate to art, music, PE, technology, the library, and so on.

❑ Reduce the number of all-staff meetings, and replace them with smaller team meetings where the topics under discussion can be tailored to the needs of the group (Pardini, 1999).

❑ Use paraprofessionals, student teachers, and aides to cover classes on a regular basis.

❑ Allocate more staff positions to classroom teaching than to pullout teaching and/or support roles (Darling-Hammond, 1999).

❑ Implement schedules that engage students with fewer teachers each day for longer periods of time (Darling-Hammond, 1999).

❑ Free teachers from nonprofessional activities (e.g., playground, bus duty, and so on).

❑ Use professional development funding and time allocation for teamwork.

AGREEMENT OF PURPOSE

A structure and process to facilitate defining shared purpose and priority goals to guide the work of a team, department, or faculty

Benefits of Shared Purpose and Priority Goals:

- Ensures that everyone agrees on the purpose and process for the work.
- Gives a context for decision making.
- Provides a yardstick to measure progress.
- Focuses collaboration and planning.

AGREEMENT OF PURPOSE WORKSHEET

1. From my point of view, the primary purpose of our school leadership team (SLT) working as a professional learning community is . . .

2. I offer the following expertise and commitment to working as an SLT and moving toward our shared purpose . . .

3. I will consider our efforts as time well spent if the following things happen in our school this year:
   (1)

   (2)

   (3)

4. Three years from now . . .

Adapted from Dietz, M. E., Green, N., Piper, J., & Williams, R. (2001). *Facilitating learning communities.* Oxford, OH: National Staff Development Council.

Facilitator Guide Example

Time	Activity	Facilitator Notes
5 min	**Welcome** **Agenda Review** Individual reflection Small-group processing Whole-group process for coming to consensus on group norms Closure **Focus Principle:** Principle 3: Collaborative teaming for teaching and learning **Objectives** Participants will: 1.1. Identify the group norms important for the group to become a high-performance team.	• Agenda and objectives are provided on the handout. • Facilitator needs to have one copy of the handout per participant. • Each small group needs sticky notes, colored markers, and worksheets. • Post chart paper with the agenda and objectives for reference to facilitate the opening.
15 min	**Grounding Activity** 2.1. Individually reflect on the following question and record your reflections on the worksheet provided. *"Think of an experience you have had when you were a member of a high-performance team. What were the behaviors and actions that contributed to the team's ability to achieve a high level of performance?"* 3.2. Read over your reflection notes and identify 3–5 behaviors or actions that you felt were critical to the team being able to be a high-performance team.	• Provide the handout for the individual reflection activity. • It is important that individuals have quiet reflection time to respond to the question. • Participants should work with people other than those whom they have chosen to sit with.

(Continued)

Time	Activity	Facilitator Notes
	4.3. Write each of these behaviors or actions on sticky notes, using one sheet per response. 5.4. Turn to your elbow partner and share your responses. 6.5. As partners, come to agreement on 2–3 behaviors or actions that you both believe are very important for a high-performance team.	
10 min for either process	**Purpose of Norms** *Norms help groups build trust by:* • Creating a climate that makes it safe to challenge • Being creative • Taking risks • Allowing for satisfying, important work to occur *Norms support the opportunity to:* • Engage in deep, insightful conversations • Listen • Help ensure time together is well spent **Processing Information** *Affinity Grouping—small-group processing* 7.1. Elbow partners team up with at least two other pairs of elbow partners and share their 2–3 sticky note responses. Once all responses have been shared, group the responses that are similar together.	• Facilitator needs to present the purpose of norms to the group. • It should be noted that norms should be arrived at through a process of consensus. • Each person must support the use of the norms as they are written; therefore, clarity of meaning and action must be ensured. • Depending on the size of the whole group, arrange in small table groups of 4–6 people. • Provide each group with sufficient sticky notes. • Ask participants to clear an area on their table for sorting and grouping their individual norms. • Post chart paper at the front of the room to collect the groups' identified norms.

Time	Activity	Facilitator Notes
	8.2. Select the statement or create a statement that captures the intent of the responses that have been grouped together.	
	9.3. Identify 2–3 statements the group most supports and write them on the chart paper at the front of the room.	

10 min	**Identifying Group Norms**
	
	10.1. Once all groups have written their statements on the chart paper, as a whole group, determine which ones are most similar.
	
	11.2. Identify 5–7 group norms that will guide the group using a **process of consensus**, which ensures that:
	
	• Everyone has had sufficient opportunity to ask clarifying questions to ensure clarity of meaning of the statement.
	
	• Everyone feels that they had an opportunity to be heard and has participated in the discussion to reach this stage of agreement.
	
	• Everyone is willing to support the statement both publicly and privately, and will demonstrate support through their actions.
	
	12.3. Check for consensus on the norm before recording on the final list.
	
	13.4. Post the List of Norms on the wall and review at the beginning of each meeting.
		• A list of 5–7 norms that are clear, focused, agreed upon, and preferably written in positive prose ("We will …," rather than "We won't …") should serve the group well.
		• If the list is too extensive, it becomes difficult to assess the effectiveness of the norms and the group's usage of them.
		• Facilitator should check that everyone agrees that consensus has been reached on each norm before recording it on the final list. **Process of consensus includes:**
		
		  ○ Everyone has had sufficient opportunity to ask clarifying questions to ensure clarity of meaning of the statement.
		  ○ Everyone feels that they had an opportunity to be heard and has participated in the discussion to reach this stage of agreement.
		  ○ Everyone is willing to support the statement both publicly and privately, and will demonstrate support through their actions.

5 min	**Closure** 14.1. Plus/Delta process	• A simple Plus/Delta process is appropriate for closure. • Invite participants to state what they felt went well with the process to identify group norms. • Invite participants to share what they feel could be improved on in the process.

TOOL E: AN EXAMPLE PARTICIPANT HANDOUT FOR CREATING GROUP NORMS

Date of session:

Agenda

- Welcome
- Individual reflection
- Small-group processing
- Whole-group process for coming to consensus on group norms
- Closure

Objectives

Participants will:

- Identify the group norms important for the group to become a high-performance team.

Individual Reflection

- Individually reflect on the following question and record your reflections.

> "Think of an experience you have had when you were a member of a high-performance team. What were the behaviors and actions that contributed to the team's ability to achieve a high level of performance?"

Consensus means:

70% agreement, but 100% support—Although you, as an individual, may not be in total agreement with the wording, you fully support its intent and agree to demonstrate that support through your actions and talk.

The **process of consensus** ensures that:

✓ Everyone has had sufficient opportunity to ask clarifying questions to ensure clarity of meaning of the statement.
✓ Everyone feels that they had an opportunity to be heard and has participated in the discussion to reach this stage of agreement.
✓ Everyone is willing to support the statement both publicly and privately, and will demonstrate support through their actions.

Group Norms	
HOPE's Meeting Norms	*7 Norms of Collaboration*
• Everyone has the right to be heard • Ideas, thoughts, and suggestions are generated with positive intentions • Starting and ending times are honored • Side conversations are avoided • Everyone focuses on group work and directions • Cell phones are on vibrate	• Pausing • Paraphrasing • Probing for specificity • Putting ideas on the table • Paying attention to self & others • Presuming positive intentions • Practicing a balance of inquiry & advocacy

Defining Indicators of Quality Instruction

Location/Date

Step 1: Brainstorm a list of observable Indicators of Quality Instruction.

1. Think of a lesson you have taught or observed that was highly successful in terms of participation and outcomes.

2. Think of these categories: teacher behaviors, student behaviors, and other indicators.

3. What were some of the key attributes of the lesson that contributed to its success in each category?

4. Individually, list teacher behaviors, student behaviors, and other indicators that you expect to see when Quality Instruction is present.

Step 2: Norm the Indicators of Quality Instruction as a group.

1. In teams or small groups, share your individual lists.

2. Combine and refine the lists to form one comprehensive list.

3. Continue combining and refining until you have a list of three to five indicators in each category (teacher behaviors, student behaviors, other indicators).

Examples of possible indicators: student engagement, exploring students' ideas, think/reflection time, inquiry, clear student expectations.

Step 3: Check Indicators of Quality Instruction.

Ensure you have distinguished between Indicators of Quality Instruction and Lesson Design/Instructional Strategies. For example, an indicator might be "student engagement" while one strategy the teacher is using to achieve engagement might be cooperative learning.

Step 4: Check for understanding by describing each Indicator of Quality Instruction.

Each indicator should have a description so that when looking for Quality Instruction, no one is confused regarding what to look for. When describing Indicators of Quality Instruction, use observational language. What does each indicator look and sound like?

Examples of Indicator descriptions of student engagement:

- The student is encouraged to participate and express ideas.
- The student is seeking to understand and asks questions.

Examples of Indicator descriptions of setting expectations:

- Students are informed regarding the objectives/standards/concepts being taught.
- Students have a clear understanding of what they are going to learn, how they will learn it, and why.

Complete Steps 5, 6, 7 on-site and prepare to share at CLA I Session 3 debriefing.

Step 5: Prepare for the Instructional Learning Walk.

1. Review the list of the Indicators of Quality Instruction and your group's description of each.

2. Identify examples of the Indicators of Quality Instruction and calibrate your group. This is done by practicing to make sure you are in alignment with each other regarding what you are looking for.

3. Record your group's Indicators of Quality Instruction on the observation sheet (Tool G).

Step 6: Do the Instructional Learning Walk.

1. Go on an Instructional Learning Walk as a group for 30 minutes.

2. Separate and walk through as many classrooms as you have time for with your Observation Sheet.

3. Look for Indicators of Quality Instruction in each classroom you visit. (This activity does not expect you to identify either the teacher or students.)

4. Place a check mark next to each indicator that you observe.

Step 7: Debrief the Instructional Learning Walk.

Tally the number of times you observed each Indicator of Quality Instruction, first individually and then as a group. Consider the following questions as a form of data.

1. Which indicators were observed most frequently?

2. Which indicators were observed least frequently?

3. Which of the indicators were observed occasionally?

OBSERVATION SHEET

To record data during Instructional Learning Walks

Check if the behavior is observed in the classroom (CR)

Indicators—Teacher behavior	*CR 1*	*CR 2*	*CR 3*	*CR 4*	*CR 5*	*CR 6*
Totals						

Indicators—Student behavior	CR 1	CR 2	CR 3	CR 4	CR 5	CR 6
Totals						

Bibliography

Bandura, A. (1977). *Social learning theory.* Englewood Cliffs, NJ: Prentice Hall.

Barth, R. S. (2001). *Learning by heart.* San Francisco, CA: Jossey-Bass.

Blankstein, A. (2004/2010). *Failure is not an option: 6 principles that guide student achievement in high-performing schools.* Thousand Oaks, CA: Corwin.

Block, P. (2008). *Community: The structure of belonging.* San Francisco, CA: Berrett-Koehler Publishers.

Bryk, A., & Schneider, B. (2002). *Trust in schools: A core resources for improvement.* New York: Russell Sage.

Bryk, A., Sebring, P. B., Allensworth, E., Luppescu, S., & Easton, J. Q. (2010). *Organizing schools for improvement: Lessons from Chicago.* Chicago: University of Chicago Press.

Cushman, K. (1995). *Making the good school better: The essential question of rigor.* Providence, RI: Coalition of Essential Schools.*Horace, 11*(4).

Csikszentmihalyi, M. (1990). *Flow: The psychology of optimal experience.* New York, NY: Harper & Row Publishers.

Darling-Hammond, L. (1999). Target time toward teachers. *Journal of Staff Development, (20)*2.

Darling-Hammond, L., Wei, R. C., Andree, A., Richardson, N., & Orphanos, S. (2009). *Professional learning in the learning profession: A status report on teacher development in the United States and abroad.* Dallas, TX: National Staff Development Council.

Day, J. C., & Newburger, E. C. (2002, July). *The big payoff: Educational attainment and synthetic estimates of work-life earnings.* Washington, DC: U.S. Census Bureau.

Deal, T. E., & Peterson, K. D. (2009). *Shaping school culture: The heart of leadership.* San Francisco, CA: Jossey-Bass.

Deming, W. E. (1982). *Out of the crisis.* Cambridge, MA: MIT Press.

Dietz, M. E., Green, N., Piper, J., & Williams, R. (2001). *Facilitating learning communities.* Oxford, OH: National Staff Development Council.

DuFour, R., & Eaker, R. (1998). *Professional learning communities at work: Best practices for enhancing student achievement.* Bloomington, IN: National Educational Service.

Eastman, C. (1902). *Indian boyhood.* New York: McClure, Phillips.

Easton, L. (1999). Tuning protocols. *Journal of Staff Development, 20*(3), 55–56.

Easton, L. (2008). *Powerful designs for professional learning* (2nd ed.) Dallas, TX: National Staff Development Council.

Elmore, R. F. (2004). *School reform from the inside out.* Cambridge, MA: Harvard Education Press.

Evans, R. (1996). *The human side of school change.* San Francisco, CA: Jossey-Bass.

Fliegel, S., & Macguire, J. (1993). *Miracle in East Harlem: The fight for choice in public education.* New York: Random House.

Friedman, T. L. (2008). *Hot, flat, and crowded: Why we need a green revolution and how it can renew America.* New York: Farrar, Straus and Giroux.

Fullan, M. (2010). *All systems go.* Thousand Oaks, CA: Corwin.

Hargreaves, A. (2010). *Leading beyond expectations: Inspiring examples of success from business, sports, and education.* Learning Forward Keynote Address, annual conference, Atlanta, GA, December 4–8.

Hargreaves, A., & Fink, D. (2004, April). The seven principles of sustainable leadership: Leading in tough times. *Educational Leadership, 61*(7), 8–13.

Hargreaves, A., & Fink, D. (2006). *Sustainability leadership*. San Francisco, CA: Jossey-Bass.

Hargreaves, A., & Shirley, D. L. (2009). *The fourth way: The inspiring future for educational change*. Thousand Oaks, CA: Corwin.

Hope Foundation Reports, www.hopefoundation.org/districtsuccess.html

Houston, P. D. (2010). *Giving wings to children's dreams: Making our schools worthy of our children*. Thousand Oaks, CA: Center for Empowered Leadership, Corwin.

Inside The Workshop Vol. 2 Issue #1 © Great Schools Workshop Inc. 2008.

Kennedy, B. P., Kawachi, I., Glass, R., & Prothrow-Stith, D. (1998). Income distribution, socioeconomic status, and self rated health in the United States: Multilevel analysis. *British Medical Journal, 317*(7163), 917–921.

King, M. L., Jr. (1963, April). Letter from Birmingham city jail: The Negro is your brother. *Liberation: An Independent Monthly, 23*, 10–16.

Lambert, L., & Gardner, M. (2009). *Women's way of leading*. Indianapolis, IN: Dog Ear Publishing.

Leithwood, K., Harris, A., & Strauss, T. (2010). *Leading school turnaround: How successful leaders transform low-performing schools*. San Francisco, CA: Jossey-Bass.

Loehr, J., & Schwartz, T. (2003). *The power of full engagement*. New York, NY: The Free Press.

Louis, K. S., Leithwood, K., Wahlstrom, K. L., & Anderson, S. E. (2010, July). *Learning from leadership: Investigating the links to improved student learning*. Report to The Wallace Foundation, University of Minnesota.

McKinsey/Organization for Economic Co-Operation and Development (OECD). (2010). *Education at a glance 2010*. Paris, France: OECD.

Moore, D., & Fendler, L. (2003). *Teaching in the knowledge society: Education in the age of insecurity*. New York, NY: Teachers College Press.

Newmann, F. M., & Wehlage, G. G. (1995). *Successful school restructuring: A report to the public and educators*. Madison: Center on Organization and Restructuring of Schools, Wisconsin Center for Education Research.

Norris, M. (2010). *All things considered: A look at race, poverty, and public education*. Keynote address at the annual conference of Learning Forward, Atlanta, GA.

Pappas, G. (2008). *John Dewey's ethical democracy as experience*. Bloomington: Indiana University Press.

Pardini, P. (1999). Making time for adult learning. *Journal of Staff Development, (20)*2.

Pascale, R., Sternin, J., & Sternin, M. (2010). *The power of positive deviance: How unlikely innovators solve the world's toughest problems*. Cambridge, MA: Harvard Business Pres.

Patterson, K., Grenny, J., Maxfield, D., McMillan, R., & Switzler, A. (2008). *Influencer: The power to change anything*. New York, NY: McGraw-Hill.

Payne, C. M. (2010). *So much reform, so little change: The persistence of failure in urban schools*. Cambridge, MA: Harvard Education Press.

Phillips, V. (2009, September). More is not better: What we need from common standards is focus and flexibility. *Education Week, 29*(5), 28.

Pink, D. H. (2009). *Drive: The surprising truth about what motivates us*. New York: Riverhead Hardcover.

Programme for International Student Assessment (PISA). (2009). *What students know and can do: Student performance in reading, mathematics and science* [Executive Summary]. Paris, France: Author.

Reeves, D. (2007). *Iowa association of school boards*. Retrieved from http://www.ia-sb.org/Publications.aspx?id=4342

Schaumburg's Results–Hope Foundation Reports, www.hopefoundation.org/districtsuccess.html. (Fort Wayne Results)

Schein, E. (2004). *Organizational culture and leadership.* (3rd ed.) San Francisco, CA: Jossey-Bass.

Schlechty, P. C. (1992). *Schools for the 21st century: Leadership imperatives for educational reform.* San Francisco, CA: Jossey-Bass.

Senge, P. (2006). *The fifth discipline: The art and practice of the learning organization.* London: Random House Business.

Sharratt, L., & Fullan, M. (2009). *Realization: The change imperative for deepening district-wide reform.* Thousand Oaks, CA: Corwin.

Singhal, A., Sternin, J., & Dura, L. (2009). *Combating malnutrition: Positive deviance grows roots in Vietnam in the land of a thousand rice fields.* British Columbia, Canada: The Communication Initiative Network.

Slavin, R. E., Madden, N. A., Dolan, L. J., Wasik, B. A., Ross, S. M., & Smith, L. J. (1994). Whenever and wherever we choose: The replication of 'Success for All.' *Phi Delta Kappan, 75*, 639–647.

Tzu, S. (2005). *The art of war.* Boston, MA: Shambhala.

Wagner, T. (2008). *The global achievement gap: Why even our best schools don't teach the new survival skills our children need—And what we can do about it.* New York: Basic Books.

Wagner, T., Kegan, R., Lahey, L. L., Lemons, R. W. Garnier, J., Helsing, D., & Rasmussen, H. T. (2005). *Change leadership: A practical guide to transforming our schools.* San Francisco, CA: Jossey-Bass.

Wilkinson, R. G., & Pickett, K. (2009). *The spirit level: Why more equal societies almost always do better.* London, UK: Bloomsbury Press.

Index

CORWIN

A SAGE Company

The Corwin logo—a raven striding across an open book—represents the union of courage and learning. Corwin is committed to improving education for all learners by publishing books and other professional development resources for those serving the field of PreK–12 education. By providing practical, hands-on materials, Corwin continues to carry out the promise of its motto: **"Helping Educators Do Their Work Better."**

The HOPE Foundation logo stands for Harnessing Optimism and Potential Through Education. The HOPE Foundation helps to develop and support educational leaders over time at district- and state-wide levels to create school cultures that sustain all students' achievement, especially low-performing students.